Philip Massinger

Twayne's English Authors Series

Arthur F. Kinney, Editor

University of Massachusetts at Amherst

TEAS 435

PHILIP MASSINGER (1583–1640)
*Posthumous engraving by Thomas Cross,
published in* Three New Players, *1655.
Reproduced courtesy of the Folger Shakespeare Library.*

Philip Massinger

By Doris Adler

Howard University

Twayne Publishers
A Division of G.K. Hall & Co. • Boston

Philip Massinger

Doris Adler

Copyright © 1987 by G.K. Hall & Co.
All Rights Reserved
Published by Twayne Publishers
A Division of G.K. Hall & Co.
70 Lincoln Street
Boston, Massachusetts 02111

Copyediting supervised by Lewis DeSimone
Book production by Elizabeth Todesco
Book design by Barbara Anderson

Typeset in 11 pt. Garamond
by Modern Graphics, Inc., Weymouth, Massachusetts

Printed on permanent/durable acid-free paper
and bound in the United States of America

Library of Congress Cataloging in Publication Data

Adler, Doris Ray.
    Philip Massinger.

    (Twaynes English authors series ; TEAS 435)
    Bibliography: p. 133
    Includes index.
    1. Massinger, Philip, 1583–1640—Criticism and
interpretation.   I. Title.   II. Series.
PR2707.A35   1987   822'.3   86-19463
ISBN 0-8057-6934-X

Contents

Editor's Note

In a major revisionary study of the Jacobean and Caroline playwright and poet Philip Massinger, Doris Adler argues that his customary reputation as a crypto-Catholic writer or an unimaginative and repetitive dramatist is thoroughly misguided, misrepresenting his purpose, his art, and his significant role in English literary history. He was instead, she claims, "a proud professional playwright in battle against those forces that threatened his age and its drama." Schooled in the art of public theaters and collaborative writing, most notably with John Fletcher, Massinger became the leading Jacobean playwright whose chief purpose was to expose the weakness and corruption of James I and his court, the threat to national security and morality in the persons of Robert Carr and the Duke of Buckingham, and the continuing decadent policies of Charles I. Massinger's plays are best read as implicit political commentary, much like the court masques of his time. Adler's case for Massinger as a political radical who used the stage for his informed and pointed commentary is widely and sometimes exhaustively documented; moreover, in reassigning the mysterious Prologue to *The Guardian* and in a major rereading of *The Roman Actor* she argues persuasively that Massinger's later years were given over to opposing William Davenant and the coterie court values that he emulated and promulgated. We have wrongly understood Massinger, she concludes, because in his time the Royalists controlled much of the theater and, in time, "Massinger's plays became the property of those he had opposed. Massinger and his art have come down to us through the hands of his enemies." Doris Adler has provided the rejuvenated Twayne English Authors Series with a substantially new assessment of a neglected major playwright that is likely to become a center of study and controversy both of Massinger and of the troubled theater of the seventeenth century.

—Arthur F. Kinney

About the Author

Doris Adler, Professor of English at Howard University, where she has taught since 1966, received her undergraduate training at Berea College and Hunter College, her M. A. and Ph. D. from Howard University, has continued her study of Renaissance literature at the Folger Shakespeare Library, and has pursued her interest in theoretical criticism at the School of Theory and Criticism.

In addition to her full-length *Thomas Dekker: A Reference Guide*, Professor Adler has published studies in both literary and theater history in *Shakespeare Quarterly, Renaissance Papers, Theatre Journal, Medieval and Renaissance Drama in England, Research Opportunities in Renaissance Drama, Selected Papers from the West Virginia Renaissance Conference*, and the *Kenyon Review*. She is, perhaps, most often remembered for her study of Elizabethan iconography, "Imaginary Toads in Real Gardens," published in *English Literary Renaissance* in 1981.

Currently preparing an extended study of the theater quarrel between Davenant and Massinger, she anticipates developing a study of the forces that determine the success or failure of revivals of Renaissance plays in the post-Renaissance theater.

Preface

Studies of Philip Massinger must begin with a disclaimer similar to that of Edwards and Gibson, "Whether Massinger owned or borrowed the very many books which the study of his plays shows him to be familiar with is impossible to say. Our ignorance about his books, like our ignorance about his marriage or his home, and our ignorance about what sort of man he was, is part of the general obscurity which surrounds the personal lives of most Tudor and Stuart dramatists."[1]

And yet, despite this admitted lack of evidence for the "sort of man he was," we find, hovering in shadowy disdain over studies of his life and art, a Massinger who seems to be a cold moralistic snob who thinks he's too good to be a mere playwright and would not dash off his poor toys if he had enough money to live otherwise. Such insubstantial ghosts are very dangerous, for once they have entered our consciousness they begin to influence our readings of the plays. And, of course, the play's the thing.

The primary aim of this study is to exorcise that ghost and recover the plays of Philip Massinger as those plays engaged and entertained Jacobean and Caroline audiences. Research in literature, as in science, is a minute examination and reexamination of existing data. The results are often revisionary, even in a nonrevisionary age. To present a new reading of existing data is not to attack other scholars, but to express active gratitude to those who have provided so much and to hope that others coming after will find this work equally useful. The records of Massinger's life and career, like the records of the theater of his day, are woefully incomplete, and a single piece of new information can demand a reordering of previously known facts. Since the last full retrospective study of the life and works of Philip Massinger, new information has been recovered that reorders and illuminates the history of both Massinger and Caroline drama.

Rather than wedging that information into a received impression of Massinger, his works, and the historical context of those works, this study seeks to assemble and interpret the information about Massinger's life, works, and their theatrical and historical context as though all that information were newly recovered and previously uninterpreted. Even though the achievement of such an innocent and newborn appraisal is not possible, since every study is in some sense determined by the limitations of its author and the hidden agenda of the age in which it is written, the attempt has solved some mysteries and posed a more attractive Massinger as an alternative to his gloomy ghost.

This study focuses on Massinger as a working member of a vital theater in a stormy age. Comparisons with other playwrights, except as such comparisons were made in his own time, are avoided. In addition, this study is less interested in who wrote which part of what play than in the accepted controlling conventions of playmaking shared by playwrights who accepted and practiced collaboration with various fellow playwrights as the normal order of the day.

Massinger's plays, on first reading, seem strange, stilted, and artificial. All plays are strange, stilted, and artificial until familiarity breeds delight. All of Massinger's independent plays are described and discussed herein, but a description or summary never substitutes for a close reading of the plays themselves. Fortunately, all Massinger's independent plays and *The Fatal Dowry*, written with Nathan Field, are accessible in *The Plays and Poems of Philip Massinger* edited by Philip Edwards and Colin Gibson, who provide critical introductions for all of the plays and a general introduction that reviews Massinger's life, career, publishing history, reputation, and stage history. I cannot begin to express my appreciation for this invaluable work.

Almost all the plays that previous scholars have attributed in part to Massinger are discussed or described, in much less detail, as those plays serve to establish and illuminate specific relationships between the stage and the age. Both *The Virgin Martyr*, written with Dekker and included in *Thomas Dekker: Dramatic Works*, edited by Fredson Bowers (Cambridge: Cambridge University Press, 1958), and *The Old Law*, edited by Catherine Shaw (New York: Garland, 1972), are included in William Gifford's nineteenth-century edition of *Plays of Philip Massinger*. Massinger's collaborations with Fletcher are available either in editions of the works of Beaumont and Fletcher or in critical editions of individual plays.

In order to establish the primary context of Massinger's plays we need to know answers to the same questions we would ask about a contemporary play or film: when and where were the plays first performed? when did they reach print? what were the other new plays performed in the same season? who were the actors? how long did the plays stay current? which old plays were still current? Many of these questions, which can be answered in a general way, automatically, about our favorite contemporary plays or films, are impossible to answer for the plays of Massinger and his contemporaries. If answers are available, those answers, in most instances, are provided by Gerald Eades Bentley in his seven-volume *The Jacobean and Caroline Stage.*[2]

Any play read in isolation from the other plays of that same moment is a play read out of a crucial context. The length of this study does not permit either the illuminating cross-reading of Massinger's plays and the plays of his colleagues and competitors or detailed illustrations from Massinger's own plays. There is no secondary substitute for reading all the plays that came to the London stage in a single year; even *Othello* or *Hamlet,* read as revivals at court in 1636, seem new and different when read in conjunction with other plays of that season.

All plays are part of the history of their age and may be a better reflection of the fears and dreams of their moment than the records of state or the chronicles of statesmen. This study, therefore, considers the plays of Massinger as small patterns in the tapestry of the time of James I and Charles I. Massinger's plays, on both stage and page, are also part of the longer history since the closing of the London theaters in 1642, but the study of that larger tapestry is left to others. Edwards and Gibson provide an excellent summary of the stage history of Massinger's plays, and Colin Gibson is preparing a full-length study of Massinger's reputation.

The inseparability of Massinger, his theater, and his age is commanding the attention of contemporary scholars in both literature and history. *Philip Massinger: A Critical Reassessment,* edited by Douglas Howard (Cambridge: Cambridge University Press, 1985), originally planned to celebrate the quartercentenary of Massinger's birth in 1983, reflects this contemporary interest in contextual reappraisal. Literary scholars, such as Philip J. Finkelpearl, are using historical evidence to challenge long-held, distorting assumptions about Jacobean and Caroline drama.[3] And, historians, such as Martin Butler, are turning to the literature of the period, particularly the dramatic literature, as powerful, albeit brief, chronicles of the age.[4]

The following pages seek to demonstrate that Massinger was,

from his early years of apprenticeship through years of triumph and decline, a proud professional playwright in battle against those forces that threatened his age and its drama.

Doris Adler

Howard University

Chronology

Plays that have been attributed to Massinger on the basis of internal evidence are indicated by a question mark; an asterisk indicates a collaborator or collaborators.

1583 Philip Massinger born, second child of Anne and Arthur Massinger; baptised in Salisbury 24 November.

1594–1599 Living in London where three sisters are born: Susan, 1594; Catherine, 1596; Barbara, 1599.

1602 Enters St. Alban Hall, Oxford, 14 May and spends some years there; does not receive a degree.

1603 Father, Arthur Massinger, dies; will proven in London 2 June.

1611? *Second Maiden's Tragedy?**

1612? *The Captain?**

1613 Tripartite letter with Nathan Field and Robert Daborne to Philip Henslowe. *Bonduca?** *The Honest Man's Fortune?**

1614? *The Faithful Friends?**

1615 4 July, signs a bond with Robert Daborne for repayment of a loan to Philip Henslowe; 23 October witnesses, along with Daborne and Henslowe, signing of three documents relating to a transaction that includes Edward Alleyn. Earliest date assigned for poem addressed to Sir William Herbert, Earl of Pembroke.

1616? *The Queen of Corinth* (1616–1618)?* *The Knight of Malta* (1616–1619)?* *The Bloody Brother, or Rollo, The Bloody Brother* (1616–1619)?* *Thierry and Theodoret* (c. 1607–1621)?*

1617? *The Jeweller of Amsterdam, or The Hague* (1616–1619), lost.*

1618? *The Old Law* (c. 1615–1618), attributed to Massinger, Thomas Middleton, and William Rowley on title page, 1656.

1619 *The Fatal Dowry* (c. 1616–1619).* *The Little French Lawyer* (1619–1623)?* *Sir John van Olden Barnavelt?* *The Laws of Candy* (1619–1623)?*

1620 *The Virgin Martyr,** licensed for the Red Bull. *Antonio and Vallia* (c. 1613–1640), lost. *Philenzo and Hypollita* (c. 1613–1640), lost. *The Custom of the Country* (1619–1623)?* *The False One* (1619–1623)?* Named by John Taylor in *The Praise of Hemp-Seed* as one of the contemporary writers of true worth.

1621 *The Woman's Plot,* lost, on list for performance at court, 27 March 1622. *The Duke of Milan* (1621–1622). *The Island Princess?** *The Double Marriage* (c. 1621)?*

1622 Poem, "A Newyeares Guift," to Lady Katherine Stanhope, Countess of Chesterfield (1621–1622). *The Sea Voyage?** *The Beggars' Bush?** *The Spanish Curate?** *The Prophetess?** *The Virgin Martyr* (1620), first quarto.

1623 *The Bondman,* 3 December, for Queen of Bohemia's Men; played at court 27 December. *The Wandering Lovers,* later known as *The Lovers' Progress?** *The Duke of Milan* (1621), first quarto; poem enclosed in a presentation copy to Sir Francis Foljambe.

1624 *The Renegado,* 17 April, *The Parliament of Love,* 3 November, both for Queen of Bohemia's Men. *The Spanish Viceroy, or The Honour of Women,* lost, performed by King's Men without license. *The Virgin Martyr* (1620), 7 July, relicensed because of new scene for his Majesty's Revels. *The Bondman* (1623), first quarto. Associated with William Bagnall in a Chancery suit against Thomas Smith and Tristram Horner.

1625 "London's Lamentable Estate," poem on plague. "The Virgin's Character" (1625–1630), poem addressed to Dorothy Knyvett, eldest daughter of Sir Philip Knyvett. *The Unnatural Combat* (1621–1625). *A New Way to Pay Old Debts* (1621?–1625?). *The Elder Brother?** *Love's Cure, or the Martial Maid?** *A Cure for a Cockold?**

1626   *The Roman Actor,* 11 October, King's Men. *The Fair Maid of the Inn?,* 22 January for King's Men.*

1627   *The Judge,* lost, 6 June for King's Men. *The Great Duke of Florence,* for Queen Henrietta's Men.

1628   *The Honour of Women,* lost, 6 May for King's Men.

1629   Named as debtor to Nathaniel Field, printer, who addresses a petition to the Lord Chamberlain 20 July. *The Picture,* 8 June for King's Men. *Minerva's Sacrifice,* lost, 3 November for King's Men. *The Roman Actor* (1626), first quarto.

1630   *The Maid of Honour* for Queen Henrietta's Men. Manuscript "Prologue" for *The Maid of Honour.* Manuscript poem, "A Charme for a Libeller." Commendatory poem to James Shirley in his *The Grateful Servant. The Picture* (1629), first quarto. *The Renegado* (1624), first quarto. Mentioned as a writer in *Elegy on Randolph's Finger.*

1631   *Believe as You List,* refused license 11 January, but on 6 May allowed for King's Men. *The Emperor of the East,* 11 March for King's Men. *The Unfortunate Piety,* lost, 13 June for King's Men. *The Virgin Martyr* (1620), second quarto. Funeral poem for Sir Warham St. Leger, buried 11 October.

1632   *The City Madam,* 25 May for the King's Men. *The Maid of Honour* (1630), first quarto. *The Emperor of the East* (1631), first quarto.

1633   *The Guardian,* 31 October for the King's Men. *A New Way to Pay Old Debts* (1625), first quarto.

1634   *The Tragedy of Cleander* (revival of *The Lovers' Progress?*), 7 May for King's Men. 13 May seen by Queen at Blackfriars. *A Very Woman,* 6 June for King's Men. *The Guardian* (1633) performed at court 12 January.

1635   *The Orator,* lost, 10 January for the King's Men. *A New Way to Pay Old Debts* (1625) performed in provinces.

1636   Poem, "Sero, Sed Serio," on the death of Charles, son of Philip Herbert, Earl of Pembroke. *The Bashful*

Lover, 9 May for the King's Men. *The Great Duke of Florence* (1627), first quarto.

1637   First performance (?) of *The Bashful Lover* licensed just before closing of theaters in 1636.

1638   *The King and the Subject*, lost, 5 June allowed for King's Men after censorship by king and a change of title. *The Bondman* (1623), second quarto. *The Duke of Milan* (1622), second quarto.

1639   *Alexius, or The Chaste Lover {Gallant}*, lost, 25 September for the King's Men. A poem, "To his Son, Upon his Minerva," addressed to James Smith and commending his "The Innovation of Penelope and Ulysses, a Mock-Poem," written in the late 1630s. *The Unnatural Combat* (1625), first quarto.

1640   *The Fair Anchoress of Pausilippo {or The Prisoner}*, lost, 26 January for the King's Men. Buried 18 March in St. Saviour's Church, Southwark.

Chapter One
Background and Biography

Family and Formative Years

Philip Massinger, baptized in the church of St. Thomas, Salisbury, 24 November 1583, was the only son of Anne and Arthur Massinger and the second of their five children. The Massinger family could trace a long and active history in the provincial life of Gloucester and in the broader concerns of England. Massinger's grandfather, William, for example, served as sheriff, alderman, and mayor of Gloucester and as a member of Parliament for that county.[1]

The playwright's father, Arthur Massinger, earned a B.A. from St. Alban Hall, Oxford, in 1571, became a fellow of Merton College, Oxford in 1573, received his M.A. from that college in 1577 and from Cambridge the following year. Arthur Massinger also accompanied Sir Humphrey Gilbert and his half brother, Sir Walter Raleigh, on an abortive expedition to the New World in 1578. By 1583 Arthur Massinger had begun his service as solicitor and trusted confidential servant to the Herbert family, first to Sir Henry Herbert, second earl of Pembroke, until his death in 1601 and then to his son and heir, Sir William Herbert, third earl of Pembroke, until 1608.[2]

During his years of service to the Herberts, powerful lords and central figures in the courts of Queen Elizabeth and King James, Arthur Massinger represented Herbert as an Examiner on the Council of Marches, served three times as a member of Parliament, delivered letters from Pembroke to the Privy Council, and helped negotiate the marriage between Pembroke's son and Burghley's granddaughter.[3]

In 1579 Arthur Massinger married Anne Crompton, the daughter of William Crompton, a mercer of Stafford and London. Thomas Crompton, Anne's brother, entered Oxford in the late 1570s when Arthur Massinger was still there, and the two families probably became acquainted at that time. Thomas Crompton, in service to the earl of Essex and representing his interests in Gloucester in the

1

1590s, became a Chancellor of the Diocese of London and judge in the court of Admiralty.[4]

By 1594, Anne and Arthur Massinger, their daughter Elizabeth (mentioned in her Grandfather Crompton's will in 1582), and their eleven-year-old son, Philip, were living in London where the births of three additional daughters are registered: Susan, 13 January 1594; Catherine, 23 December 1596; and Barbara, 3 January 1599.

In May 1602, young Philip Massinger entered St. Alban Hall, Oxford, but did not take a degree. According to Wood, "tho incouraged in his studies by the Earl of *Pembroke*, yet, he applied his mind more to Poetry and Romances for about four years or more, than to Logick and Philosophy, which he ought to have done, and for that end was patronized." Langbaine, however, reports that Massinger was sent to the university by his father and that he "closely pursued his Studies . . . for Three or Four years space."[5] Since Massinger's father died 4 June 1603, Langbaine's account is, perhaps, more accurate; Massinger may have been unable to remain at the university because of either financial reasons or family obligations.

Perhaps Philip and his uncle, Richard Massinger, who was present when his brother's will was proved, took Philip's mother and sisters back to Gloucester to live. Richard Massinger's will was proved in Gloucester in 1608, and inscriptions in the Cathedral Church of Gloucester indicate that Anne Massinger died in that city at seventy on 21 October 1636 and that her daughter Elizabeth died there at seventy-three in 1665. In addition to these suggestions that Philip Massinger had long and enduring ties to the Gloucester community, he also seems to have remained on close terms with his "kinsman" William Singleton, who was member of Parliament from Gloucester, an alderman for that city, and a captain in their forces against the king during the English Civil War.[6] Speculate as one may, however, there are no records of Philip Massinger's life beyond those already cited until 1613 by which time he had become a playwright, was collaborating on some unknown play with John Fletcher, Nathan Field, and Robert Daborne, and was in prison for debt.[7]

Despite the lack of evidence about Massinger's early life, a familiar shortcoming in the study of so many poets and playwrights of the period, many have been tempted to weave a fantastic biographical scenario on this slender frame of facts. But evidence provides no suggestion that Massinger shared in the aristocratic life of the Herberts at Wilton. Rather, evidence does suggest that his childhood and youth were spent in an educated family that was substantially involved in provincial government, a family that worked for, rubbed shoulders with, and presumably shared the values of the greatest courtiers of the court of Queen Elizabeth. Massinger's life, like the life of the nation, changed abruptly in 1603 when Queen Elizabeth died, plague ravaged London, and King James I set out from Scotland to claim the throne of England. For Massinger the national loss and change was compounded by personal loss and change; his father died, his mother was left with four dependent daughters, three of them young children, and Massinger became head of the family. No one knows how he began his career as a playwright.

Early Years in the Theater

The evidence for an account of Massinger's long period of theatrical apprenticeship is as scant as that for an accurate account of his formative years; the most helpful information did not become public, to the best of our knowledge, until 1658, eighteen years after Massinger's death, when Sir Aston Cokayne revealed that Massinger had collaborated on many of the plays attributed to Beaumont and Fletcher.[8] On the basis of this information, generations of scholars have assumed that Massinger became Fletcher's primary collaborator after Beaumont married and retired from the theater in 1613. In addition, Massinger, Nathan Field, and Robert Daborne, in prison for debt in 1613, addressed a tripartite letter to Philip Henslowe asking him for a loan and assuring him that it would be repaid from the play they were writing with Fletcher. Scholars have logically concluded that Massinger began his collaboration with Fletcher before the date of the letter, perhaps as early as 1607–9.

The letter to Henslowe, read in the light of Massinger's later career, provides valuable information about Massinger's theatrical affiliations and associations. The letter is addressed to Philip Henslowe, manager of Lady Elizabeth's Company, a company that, in its various forms, commanded Massinger's services for many years. After the original company disbanded, a number of the members were absorbed into a new company, also called Lady Elizabeth's, or the Queen of Bohemia's Company, managed by Christopher Beeston at the Phoenix (also known as the Cockpit); at a later period, this company formed the nucleus of Queen Henrietta's Company, also managed by Beeston at the Phoenix. Massinger seems to have begun his career writing for Lady Elizabeth's Company. Later he provided at least three independent plays for the Queen of Bohemia's Company, and at least an equal number for Queen Henrietta's Company.[9]

In addition to writing plays from 1613 to at least 1630 for that contiguous group of actors that became Queen Henrietta's Company, Massinger also wrote for and perhaps became acquainted with other actors who were members of Lady Elizabeth's Company in 1613 and, later, principal players with the King's Men. Joseph Taylor, for example, who played the leading role in Massinger's *The Roman Actor* and wrote commendatory verse for the quarto of that play, began his acting career with Lady Elizabeth's, joined the King's Men in 1619, and became one of the managers of that company at about the same time that Massinger became a primary playwright for the King's Men.[10]

Massinger's early collaboration with Field, Daborne, and Fletcher, evident from the tripartite letter, continued and flourished with Field and Fletcher, as later evidence confirms. Although only the initials "P. M. and N. F." appear on the 1632 title page of *The Fatal Dowry,* Massinger acknowledged his authorship by including the play in a collection known today as the Harbord volume, a group of eight that he evidently planned to publish as a collection,[11] and evidence strongly suggests that Nathan Field was his collaborator. Scholars who have addressed the attribution of shares in the Beaumont-Fletcher canon have found the hands of both Field and Massinger in several of those plays. Robert Daborne, on the contrary, disappeared from the world of the theater only a few years after he, Field, Fletcher, and Massinger collaborated on some unidentified play. There is no external evidence that Massinger and Daborne worked together on other plays, but he has been suggested as a possible collaborator for several early ones.

Massinger seems to have been better paid and, therefore, more highly valued than Daborne, who asked in another letter to Henslowe that he add ten shillings to his payment that it might equal Massinger's. Two years later both Daborne and Massinger were evidently still working for Henslowe, still turning to him for loans, still fighting the poverty endemic to Henslowe's playwrights. On 4 July 1615 Daborne and Massinger signed a bond to repay a small loan from Henslowe.[12] In this same year or shortly thereafter Massinger made a bid for patronage, a playwright's only means of gaining both the time and the support necessary to create those plays that might establish a reputation, demand a decent price, and furnish release from the treadmill of endless collaboration, revision of old plays, and patching out one-day-wonders on assignment.

Massinger, not illogically, turned to the new Lord Chamberlain, Sir William Herbert, and recalled the former service of his father. Although there is no evidence that Massinger's pleading poem served his purpose, it does provide some evidence of his attitude about obsequious flattery and self-praise, his early work, and its anonymity:

> I would not for a pension or A place
> Part soe wth myne owne Candor; lett me rather
> Liue poorely on those toyes I would not father,
> Not knowne beyond A Player or A Man
> That does pursue the course that I haue ran,
> Ere soe grow famous.[13]

Massinger evidently considered many of the plays he wrote on assignment "toyes" that he would not have chosen to write and that no one knew he had written except the actors and those fellow playwrights engaged in the same occupation — those that "pursue the course that I haue ran."

Massinger continued in that course for five years without leaving more than a trace of his name in the theater records that survive. Despite the lack of surviving records, however, Massinger seems to have been known by his contemporaries. John Taylor's *The Praise of Hemp-seed*, 1620, includes Massinger in a prestigious group:

> And many there are liuing at this day
> Which do in paper there true worth display:
> As *Dauis, Drayton,* and the learned *Dun,*
> *Ionson,* and *Chapman, Marston, Middleton,*
> With *Rowlye, Fletcher, Withers, Messenger,*
> *Heywood,* and all the rest where e're they are,
> Must say their lines, but for the paper sheete
> Had scarcely ground, whereon to set their feete.

No one knows which plays were known as Massinger's in 1620 or what works served as the basis of his reputation at that time. Subsequent scholars, however, knowing he had a share in the Beaumont-Fletcher canon and assuming he replaced Beaumont in 1613 or 1614 as Fletcher's primary collaborator, have given Massinger a share of many of the most popular plays of his time and some of the most enduring in our own.

Massinger's Collaborations

Massinger began writing shares of plays at some undetermined time before 1613 and continued until Fletcher's death in 1625. Even after that date he seems to have completed plays left unfinished by Fletcher and to have revised old plays written wholly or in part by him. Of the many plays attributed to Massinger in part, only two can be confirmed as his on the basis of unquestioned external evidence. Massinger's joint authorship of *The Fatal Dowry,* as noted earlier, is confirmed by the initials on the title page and its inclusion in the Harbord volume. The collaboration of Massinger and Thomas Dekker on *The Virgin Martyr* is confirmed by their names on the title page of the 1622 quarto and a subsequent edition reprinted in Massinger's lifetime. *The Old Law* (c. 1615–18), according to the title page of the first quarto in 1656, was written by Philip Massinger, Thomas Middleton, and William Rowley. However, despite this evidence and Gifford's inclusion of the work in Massinger's canon, the attribution of any part of that play to Massinger is generally questioned.

There is external evidence, suspect in most cases, for Massinger's authorship of a number of plays that are now lost. In 1653 Humphrey Moseley entered a long list of plays in the Stationers' Register in order to protect his copyright. Many of Massinger's known titles are included, but most of them are listed with an alternate title that is, or may be, the title of another play. It is generally agreed, as Edwards and Gibson note, that Moseley was "engaged in a delicate piece of fraud, securing his copyright for two plays for the price of one."[14] However, the previous existence of some of the plays listed as alternate titles is confirmed by the presence of their titles in other records. Moseley entered an additional list of single titles in 1660; some of the titles duplicate the previous list, and some are new.

In 1654 Moseley entered *The Jeweller of Amsterdam or The Hague* in the Stationers' Register as a play by Fletcher, Field, and Massinger, and the entry is generally accepted as evidence of a now-lost play for the King's Men (1616–17?). Both *Antonio and Valia* and *Philenzo and Hypollita,* the first listed as a comedy and the second as a tragicomedy in Moseley's list of 1660, bear names similar to titles of plays listed without an author in Henslowe's diary for 1594–95, when Massinger was too young to be writing for the theater. Whether Massinger revised old plays, possibly written by Dekker, or whether he wrote plays with similar titles is not known. Three titles that appear in Moseley's lists are mentioned in records for Massinger's active theatrical years. *The Woman's Plot*, listed by Moseley as the alternate title for *The Very Woman* in his 1653 list and separately as a comedy in his 1660 list, is included in a warrant of 27 March 1622 for payment of plays presented at court. *The Spanish Viceroy*, listed by Moseley as the alternate title for *The Honour of Women* in 1653, was played without license by the King's Men in 1624, and Sir Henry Herbert recorded a letter of apology from the King's Men in his copybook in connection with a similar offense in 1633. *The Honour of Women*, listed by Moseley as an alternate title for *The Spanish Viceroy* in 1653 and separately as a comedy in 1660, was licensed by Herbert for the King's Men 6 May 1628. According to Bentley, Malone thought this title was a mistake and should have been *The Maid of Honour*.

The only external evidence for assigning any part of the Beaumont and Fletcher canon to Massinger is Cokayne's claim, but there is no reason to question that claim since Fletcher regularly worked with a collaborator and Massinger seems a logical successor to Beaumont. In lieu of external evidence, scholars since the beginning of the nineteenth century have relied on various systems of internal evidence of style or linguistic patterns to determine which portions of which plays of the Beaumont and Fletcher canon were written by Massinger.[15] Turning their attention to that first collection of Beaumont and Fletcher plays, many of which cannot be dated with any degree of accuracy and all printed for the first time in 1647, scholars have attributed the following plays, in part, to Massinger: *The Captain* (1609–12?), *Bonduca* (1609–14?), *The Honest Man's Fortune* (1613), *The Queen of Corinth* (1616–17), *The Knight of Malta* (1616–18), *The Little French Lawyer* (1619–23), *The Laws of Candy* (1619?), *The Custom of the Country* (c. 1619–23), *The Double Marriage*, (c. 1621), *The False One* (c. 1620), *The Island Princess* (1619–21), *The Sea Voyage* (1622), *The Prophetess* (1622), *The Beggars' Bush* (1622), *The Spanish Curate* (1622), *The Lovers' Progress* (or *The Wandering Lovers*, or *Cleander*, or *Lisander and Calista*) (1623, revised 1634?), *Love's Cure, or The Martial Maid* (1625?), *The Fair Maid of the Inn*, (1625/ 26). While scholars are in agreement about the assignment of shares for some of these plays, they disagree about others and about the contributions of collaborators other than Fletcher and Massinger, particularly in discussions of the plays written before 1620. [16]

In addition to attributing to Massinger shares of the plays printed in the first Beaumont-Fletcher collection, scholars have also determined that Massinger had a hand in several other plays, some printed during his lifetime, some after the closing of the theaters, and some remaining in manuscript until the nineteenth or twentieth century. *Rollo, Duke of Normandy, or The Bloody Brother* (1617?; revised 1627–30?) appears without an accompanying author's name in the records of several performances during the Caroline years. The attribution in the 1639 entry in the Stationers' Record is "I: B:"; on the 1639 title page it is "B. J. F."; and on the 1640 title page it is John Fletcher. J. D. Jump summarizes the problem in the title of his 1948 edition of the play: *Rollo Duke of Normandy or The Bloody Brother, A Tragedy, Attributed to John Fletcher, George Chapman, Ben Jonson and Philip Massinger.*

The publication history of *Thierry and Theodoret* (1607?–21), also attributed in part to Massinger, is similar. First printed as an anonymous play in 1621, it was attributed to John Fletcher in the 1648 edition, and to Beaumont and Fletcher in the 1649 edition. On the other hand Fletcher's name is included in the entry in the Stationers' Register, on the title page of both 1637 editions, and in the prologue and epilogue of *The Elder Brother* (1625), but there is widespread agreement that Massinger had a hand in this play. There is far less agreement that Massinger had a share in *The Cure for a Cuckold* (1624–25) attributed to John Webster and William Rowley on the title page of the first edition in 1661. The similarity of this play and Massinger's *The Parliament of Love*, however, is generally recognized.

Three plays left in manuscript for centuries are included in Massinger's canon of collaborations. The manuscript of *The Faithful Friends* (c. 1614–21?), included in Moseley's list of 1660 as a play by Beaumont and Fletcher and printed for the first time in Alexander Dyce's edition of their works in 1812, is written in several hands, one of which has been identified as Massinger's. There is no external evidence for the authorship of *Sir John van Olden Barnavelt* (1619) that remained in manuscript until A. H. Bullen published it in *A Collection of Old English Plays* in 1883, but scholars generally agree that it is the work of Fletcher and Massinger. Massinger is generally accepted as one of the authors of *The Second Maiden's Tragedy* (1611/12?) that reached print for the first time in Anne Lancaster's 1978 edition, and Bentley considers it probable that Massinger's lost play, *The Tyrant,* included in Moseley's 1660 list, is another name for that play.

In addition to writing plays with Fletcher, Field, Dekker, and others, Massinger emerged as a recognized independent playwright sometime around 1620 and, from that time until shortly after Fletcher's death in 1625, he seems to have divided his time and service between the King's Men, for whom he wrote at least two independent plays in addition to his many collaborations with Fletcher, and the Queen of Bohemia's Men, for whom he wrote at least two and possibly as many as four plays.

Massinger's Jacobean Plays

There is no external evidence for the exact date of composition or first performance of either *The Duke of Milan* or *The Unnatural Combat,* the two plays Massinger wrote for the King's Men during the period when his primary service to that company seems to have been his collaboration with Fletcher. Since *The Duke of Milan* was published in 1623 and the title page indicates that it was performed by "his Maiesties seruants, at the blacke Friers," Massinger must have written the play sometime before that date, probably in 1621 or 1622. *The Unnatural Combat* did not reach print until 1639, many years, it seems, after its initial performance. The title page indicates that the play was performed by the King's Men at the Globe, and Massinger refers to the play as "this old Tragedie" in his dedication.

Two of the plays Massinger wrote for the Queen of Bohemia's Men at the Phoenix can be very accurately dated. *The Bondman,* licensed for that company on 3 December 1623, played at court on 27 December 1623 and, according to the dedication to the 1624 edition, won the approval of Sir Philip Herbert, the earl of Montgomery. Sir Philip Herbert may have become Massinger's patron at this time, for, according to Aubrey, Herbert gave Massinger a small pension which after his death was paid to his wife who "lived at Cardiffe, in Glamorganshire."[17] Aubrey's statement is the only indication that Massinger ever married; nothing more is known about his family life.

On 17 April 1624 *The Renegado* was licensed for the Queen of Bohemia's Company, but it was not published until 1630. In the same year *The Virgin Martyr* was relicensed because of the addition of a scene for his Majesty's Revels at the Red Bull. There are no records of a license, however, either for *The Maid of Honour* or *A New Way to Pay Old Debts* although both, according to their title pages, were performed at the Phoenix.

Edwards and Gibson consider *The Maid of Honour* to be Massinger's first independent play and believe that it was written in 1621–22 before Sir Henry Herbert became Master of the Revels and began to keep records of licenses for new plays. Eva Bryne, in the introduction to her edition of the play, believes the play belongs to 1623, and S. R. Gardiner thinks the play was performed in 1631, the year before the first quarto of 1632. However, when these conclusions were drawn, they did not know of the existence of a manuscript prologue written for a performance of *The Maid of Honour* in 1630, a prologue that Peter Beal discovered and published for the first time in 1980. The opening lines read as follows:

Prologue to ye Mayde of honour

To all [that] are come hither, and
  haue brought
noe expectacon beyond the thought
of power in our performance; that
  this day
looke for noe mor, nor lesse, then
  a newe play
May giue satisfaccon for; a free
and happie welcome. May such
  euer bee
feasted with rarities.[18]

This would certainly seem to indicate that *The Maid of Honour* was a new play in 1630 and belongs to a later period in Massinger's career.

There is no license nor long-lost prologue to help establish the initial date for *A New Way to Pay Old Debts*. The play was not printed until 1633. Some think the play was as early as 1621; others think it was later, in 1624 or perhaps 1625. Its provincial setting and the simplicity of the staging invite one to speculate that the play was written for and initially performed in the provinces following the death of King James in 1625 when the theaters were closed because of the plague.

However, one of the main reasons for assigning *A New Way to Pay Old Debts* to a date prior to 1626 is the long-held assumption that after Fletcher's death in August 1625 Massinger became the main playwright for the King's Men and was under some agreement or contract to write exclusively for them. Until the recovery of evidence that *The Maid of Honour* was written for the Phoenix five years after the death of Fletcher, Massinger seemed to have had only one new play, *The Great Duke of Florence* (1627), performed at the Phoenix after 1625, and many have assumed that this play was in fulfillment of a prior agreement, or already written for the Queen of Bohemia's Men before Massinger assumed Fletcher's position with the King's Men. Now that it is known that Massinger had a new play for the Phoenix in 1627 and another in 1630, that old assumption must be questioned. It is quite possible that Massinger had no binding agreement with the King's Men, and that he continued for several years to write plays for both companies as he had before Fletcher's death. If he continued to write for both companies after 1625, then *A New Way to Pay Old Debts* could have been written for the Phoenix after 1625. It is possible that *A New Way to Pay Old Debts*, like *The Maid of Honour*, is a Caroline rather than a Jacobean play.

Massinger's Caroline Plays

Massinger's first play for the King's Men under Charles I was *The Roman Actor*, licensed 11 October 1626. In the dedication to the play, printed in 1629, Massinger wrote that he "euer held it the most perfit birth of my Minerua." Over the next three years Massinger had four plays licensed for the King's Men, but only *The Picture*, licensed 8 June 1629, is extant. *The Judge*, 6 June 1627, *The Honour of Women*, 6 May 1628, and *Minerva's Sacrifice*, 3 November 1629, are all lost.

In this same period Massinger wrote at least two plays for Queen Henrietta's Men at the Phoenix. *The Great Duke of Florence* was licensed in 1627 and printed in 1636, and *The Maid of Honour* was performed in 1630 and printed in 1632.

In 1631 Massinger had difficulty with the censor and, conse-

quently, made *Believe as You List* one of the most valued documents
in the annals of English drama. The original play had dramatized
the tragic encounter of Sebastian of Portugal and the king of Spain.
Herbert refused to license the play because of the peace declared
between England and Spain. Massinger simply changed the names
of the characters and the time and place of the action and resubmitted
the play; and Herbert allowed it. Massinger never released the play
for publication, and the manuscript has survived with his changes
in his own hand, with Herbert's notes and permission, and with
stage directions and actors' names written in another hand. The
manuscript, available in a facsimile edition, allows one to look over
Massinger's shoulder and watch him choose a new name with the
same number of syllables as Sebastian, mark through the old name,
and replace it with the new—and not catch every instance. Our
understanding of the reasons for censorship, of the workings of a
prompter's script, and of the shaping of material into drama owes
much to the survival of the manuscript of *Believe as You List*.

After 1630, all of Massinger's plays were written for the King's
Men. In 1631, in addition to *Believe as You List*, Massinger wrote
The Emperor of the East, printed the following year, and *The Unfortunate Piety*, now lost. By 1636 he had written all of his surviving
plays: *The City Madam*, 25 May 1632; *The Guardian*, 31 October
1633; *A Very Woman*, 6 June 1634, described in the prologue as a
revision of an earlier play yet to be identified; and *The Bashful Lover*,
9 May 1636. From 1634 until 1640 Massinger wrote at least five
plays that have not survived. *The Tragedy of Cleander*, 7 May 1634,
was seen by Queen Henrietta Maria at Blackfriars on 13 May of
that year. This play is probably a revision of *The Lovers Progress* in
the Beaumont and Fletcher canon. Nothing is known about *The
Orator*, 10 January 1635, or *Alexius, or The Chaste Lover*, 25 September 1639, or *The Fair Anchoress of Pausilippo*, 26 January 1640,
except the titles and the dates on which they were licensed.

A little more is known about the lost play *The King and the Subject*,
licensed on 5 June 1638 on the condition that the title be changed
and the reformations made by Herbert be most strictly observed.
Again Massinger had run afoul of the censor. In this instance King
Charles himself had read over the play, taken offense at a passage
about a tyrant's way of raising money, and insisted, "This is too
insolent, and to be changed." Herbert wrote out the passage in his
record book "for ever to bee remembered by my son and those that

cast their eyes on it, in honour of Kinge Charles." The seven lines copied out by Herbert are all that remain of the play.

From the death of Queen Elizabeth through the first fifteen years of King Charles I, the life of Philip Massinger seems to exist only in theater records and in the surviving plays those records address. When one seeks the breathing man behind those plays, one finds only the professional playwright addressing his patrons, his fellow playwrights, his audience, and his age. Massinger's biography is his work. All that breathes have a brief life; few survive in so much for so long.

Massinger seems to have died as he lived. According to Anthony à Wood, "he made his last exit very suddenly, in his house on the Bank-side in Southwark, near to the then playhouse, for he went to bed well and was dead before morning. Whereupon his body, being accompanied by comedians, was buried about the middle of the ch. yard belonging to S. Saviours church."[19]

The drama of Philip Massinger's life seems to have been acted out always near the playhouse accompanied by the comedians who brought his plays to life. Thus only a close study of his plays in the context of his theater can provide even a true glimmer of Philip Massinger.

Chapter Two

The Plays of Massinger's Apprenticeship, 1607–1620

Imagine discovering that a famous contemporary playwright or screenwriter had written unidentified portions of dozens of familiar plays or films before he became well known. Imagine the delight in turning back to those works of his anonymous apprenticeship and searching out early shadows of works yet to come. Then conjure up all the considerations, explanations, and rationalizations attendant on incorporating that early work into a study of his major works. "Remember, he didn't have the final say." "You have to understand, it was wartime." "It was a successful formula. No one could change it." "The cigarette in one hand and the martini in the other spelled sophistication; everyone used it." In other words, to understand, fully, the achievement or shaping powers of any playwright's apprenticeship, it is imperative to know all the mutable demands of that moment in his time, all the other plays that addressed and expressed that time, and all the traditions, conventions, and assumptions of the theater that either brought plays to life or doomed them to oblivion. It may be imperative, but it is also impossible in any study that must be primarily concerned with the major achievements of a playwright.

Although it would be ideal to have a summary of each of the nineteen plays that represent the work of Massinger's apprenticeship and an appraisal of each play in relation to the historical moment of its composition, to other plays of that moment, and to Massinger's later plays, such an ideal is unattainable in a study of this length. Therefore the nineteen plays variously attributed to Massinger are discussed here as a group that must serve as representative of Massinger before 1620. The principles of dramatic structure, the generalizations about the relation of plays to their moment of presentation, and the awareness of conventions and concerns, drawn from and illustrated by the plays of Massinger's apprenticeship, are central to an understanding of his independent, mature art.

Expectations of Jacobean-Caroline Audience

An examination of the plays of Massinger's apprenticeship and those of his professional maturity must begin by challenging some long-held assumptions and replacing those assumptions with more viable, realistic theories. The first and longest-held assumption is that Beaumont, Fletcher, Massinger, and all their fellow writers for the King's Men were Cavalier dramatists who sided with and supported the cause of Charles I and the Royalists in the English Civil War. This deeply entrenched and distorting assumption has gone unchallenged until very recently despite the fact that both Beaumont and Fletcher died before Charles I came to the throne.[1] Although he lived and wrote during the reign of Charles I, even Massinger died before the outbreak of the Civil War. Martin Butler in *Theatre and Crisis, 1632–1642*, challenging the claim that there was a Cavalier drama even as late as the 1630s, points out the following:

In 1647, the royalist publisher Humphrey Moseley issued a collected edition of Beaumont and Fletcher plays, prefacing them with thirty-seven sets of commendatory verses, many of them solicited from prominent Cavaliers. . . . These were conscious acts of propaganda . . . [that] reflect the attitude of Civil War Oxford, not peace time London, but it was very useful to Moseley to be able to suggest that such division between loyal and disloyal subjects had always been there. . . . I shall be arguing that the political possibilities of the period were much more various than the simple Cavalier-puritan-polarization allows for, and that by trying to distinguish Cavaliers from Roundheads in the 1630s we are applying categories that will not fit, looking for the conflicts of the Civil War in a decade that was not yet fighting them. And we are missing the really interesting conflicts that actually *were* there.[2]

Butler's thoroughly documented challenge to the assumptions held about Caroline drama affords an even stronger challenge to similar assumptions held about Jacobean drama.

In other words, it is not only a distorting anachronism to consider Jacobean plays as Cavalier, Royalist, or Puritan, but it is also invalid to read the plays of one time in terms of historical events yet to come. Furthermore, even though the plays under consideration here, like so many others, seem to be the very "abstract and brief chronicles of the time," it is a serious distortion of both plays and playwrights to assume that plays were written by party men for purposes of propaganda. The primary purpose of playwrights, actors, and acting companies has always been to attract and satisfy the audience. If a play preaches or propagandizes, then it does so because audiences have shown their delight in sermons or propaganda, not because a playwright is a preacher or a propagandist. The drama of every period reveals more about the tastes, concerns, and beliefs of the audience than it does about the life, beliefs, attitudes, or aspirations of the playwrights.

It is important, therefore, to look at the plays of both Massinger's apprenticeship and his professional maturity in terms of the times in which they were written and performed and in terms of the expectations, tastes, concerns, and beliefs of the audiences of those years. First of all, since the King's Men performed at the Globe, Blackfriars, and at court, the audiences for these plays were widely diversified. In addition, Massinger also wrote plays, or shares of plays, for other companies with even more diversified audiences. Therefore, the plays must be assumed to have addressed groundlings, citizens, gentry, and aristocrats.

Second, and a corollary of the first, if the plays of the period seem to advocate certain general principles, seem to address particular problems, seem to attack particular abuses, then the audience as a whole must have enjoyed the dramatization of those general principles and must have assumed that such problems and abuses were legitimately, even enjoyably, subject to dramatic attack. It is quite likely, then as now, that being part of the problem or being guilty of a particular abuse does not preclude one's enjoyment of a dramatic attack on that problem or abuse. Indeed, this seems to be in the traditional nature of drama and the primary purpose of dramatic satire. Although the didactic function of satire is ostensibly to effect change by persuading one either to identify with the victim or to face one's untenable role as an abuser, the more prevalent function may well be to provide a moment of comforting and justifying escape; the tension of repressed guilt is relieved by the two-hour traffic of the stage. One happily boos the villain and then goes back to being the villain with an easier conscience. In other words, all classes of the diversified audience of the plays of Massinger and his contemporaries seem to have enjoyed the celebration of particular virtues and allusions to and attacks on contemporary vices.

A more specific taste of the Jacobean audience was the expectation of and delight in the deep didactic concern for the salvation of man's soul and the related fate of the nation. It is too often assumed that the taste that created and perpetuated the morality play died with the first dramatization of a recognizably realistic character engaged in a more or less Aristotelian plot. Not only did morality plays and interludes continue to be performed and printed throughout the period, but, as many studies have shown, the substance and structure of the debate between the realized abstractions of good and evil continued to inform the more realistic drama until the closing of the theaters and perhaps beyond. Just as an audience today accepts the dramatic dictum that "crime doesn't pay" as a convention of popular drama, so the seventeenth-century audience expected drama, no matter how bawdy or frivolous, to argue a moral principle. A taste for the dramatic reenactment of the moral struggle of both man and nation was indigenous to the Jacobean and Caroline audience.

Before the taste for the moral struggle in drama can be fully understood by the present-day reader, however, one must see not only the Jacobean-Caroline delight in the barely submerged morality debate, but also their methods of reading such debates. On the surface, contemporary allusions and associations invited the audience to read the fiction of the play in juxtaposition to the reality of life outside the theater. But the habit of analogy was much stronger, much more conscious in the seventeenth century than it is in the twentieth, and Jacobean-Caroline audiences saw analogies between the artificial plots and characters of the stage and the real events and situations of life outside the theater with an automatic facility that cannot be easily reconstructed by the present-day reader. And, in addition, the Jacobean-Caroline audience not only saw their plays analogically, they saw them allegorically. They not only saw the artificial actions on the stage as analogues of familiar contemporary actions offstage, but they also saw the plays as emblems or allegories of the deeper patterns of morality that control the fate of a people and their native land.

The Jacobean-Caroline audience, like us, went to the theater to be entertained, and also, like us, enjoyed the pure or impure escape of make-believe. But in addition, the Jacobean-Caroline audience expected to be entertained by plot, character, music, dancing, bawdry, gossip, morality debates, analogues with contemporary situations, and emblems of the times as those times might affect the future.

Although these are the main principles to keep in mind as one turns to an examination of the plays, there is one further consideration. If the plays were to please their audiences with presentation of current concerns, particularly if such presentations were to dramatize problems central to man's soul and state, the plays had to avoid the censorship attendant on both performance and printing. Some of the familiar methods of avoiding censorship include the use of classical or otherwise familiar material to serve as an analogue for a contemporary situation; the use of stock types and conventions that provide a vocabulary of situations and characterizations that can be safely drawn upon in every age; the use of archetypal patterns; the use of a combination of attributes that both suggest and deny association with a particular person or situation; and an artificial exaggeration that protects the realistic.

These principles of reading the plays in the context of their particular moment rather than with the hindsight of history, of trying to recognize the expectations of the audience of that moment, and of reading the plays both analogically and allegorically are necessary for an understanding of both the plays associated with Massinger's apprenticeship and the plays of his professional maturity.

Early Collaborations, 1609–1614

The five plays, *Bonduca, Thierry and Theodoret, The Second Maiden's Tragedy, The Captain,* and *The Honest Man's Fortune,*[3] associated with the earliest years of Massinger's apprenticeship, provide some illustration of the controlling concerns and methods of the Jacobean theater in those years during which Massinger learned to meet the expectations of his audience. All except the last of these plays seem to have been written before the death of Prince Henry, the great hope of England, and seem to reflect the same concerns and employ the same methods as many other plays of the period.

Bonduca (c. 1609–14) harks back to the ancient chronicle history of Britain for its tragic story and dramatizes both the noble qualities of manly valor in service to the tender youth of the vulnerable heir and the tragic loss of heir and country when those noble qualities and that manly valor are forced to serve the false values of an absolute queen. Among the other plays recorded for the first decade of the reign of James I a surprising number, in like fashion, draw on similar sources, celebrate the stalwart soldier in service to timeless verities rather than to absolutist expediency, and include the threat to or loss of a young, true, noble heir.

Some of the titles that suggest similar sources and/or include similar matter and treatment of that matter are Dekker's *Sir Thomas Wyatt* (1604), Shakespeare's *King Lear* (1606), Beaumont's *Madon, King of Britain* (1606), Dekker's *The Whore of Babylon* (1607), Rowley's *The Birth of Merlin* (1608), and Shakespeare's *Cymbeline* (1610). All of these plays, like *Bonduca*, came to the stage during those years when the court of James celebrated the vain fopperies of an age of new men risen to power by their appeal to the tastes of a pleasure-loving king who feared even the sharp edge of a dinner knife. No one seems to have objected to that court and its values more than the chaste, militant young Prince Henry who defiantly protected that stalwart, imprisoned emblem of a time past, Sir Walter Raleigh.

The people of England adored Prince Henry, and both their hopes that he would usher in a new heroic age and their fears that all might be lost before he could come to the throne are dramatized in the nostalgia and the warnings of these plays. The use of ancient British matter reflects the rejection of new Scottish manners and a deep desire to return to celebrated values. The dramatized tragic mistakes of past overweening pride and wrongheadedness serve as warning to a present age. The staged threats to or loss of a young and vulnerable heir emphasize the fragility of the slender thread of hope in a day when the people looked to Prince Henry and the court looked to James's new and pampered favorite of the moment. If, as most agree, *Bonduca* was first staged between 1609 and 1611, then *Bonduca*, like *The Winter's Tale*, prophetically portrayed the death of a young and promising heir to the throne.

Thierry and Theodoret and *The Second Maiden's Tragedy*, both extremely sensational and highly artificial, include devastating portraits of favorites, tyrants, good counselors rejected or destroyed, and good stalwart soldiers made victims to the times. In addition to many apparent allusions to specific persons and events of the moment and invitations to draw analogies between the fictions on the stage and the realities outside the theater, both plays employ an allegorical method that is central to the drama that follows.

The timeless association of the sustaining native land itself with a pure, noble, faithful woman—an association apparent in the expression "Mother Nature"—had been powerfully reinforced and given particular literary currency during the reign of Elizabeth, particularly by poet Edmund Spenser who set forth both the land

and the lady who ruled the land in a series of allegorical portraits: Gloriana, Belphoebe, and Britomart among others. In addition, the perhaps equally timeless representation of a happy kingdom by the depiction of the union of a chaste, noble bride and a valiant, noble husband—a union that serves as an emblem of the good land well governed—had received political as well as literary reinforcement by both Elizabeth and James. Elizabeth claimed her people and her land as spouse and children, and James said, "I am the Husband, and the whole Isle is my lawful Wife."[4]

The repeated and varied representation of the rivalry of a true, valiant hero and a false, villainous tyrant for the possession of a noble, beautiful, chaste heroine in the plays of both the Jacobean and Caroline periods, a representation that is particularly vivid in *The Second Maiden's Tragedy,* must surely be read as an allegory of both the deep hope of the English people that their land would find its good government and their deep fears that their land might be lost to destructive leadership. The allegorical nature of this triangle is emphasized in *The Second Maiden's Tragedy* by the designation of the three central figures as Tyrant, Lady, and Govianus (son of Jove) and by the macabre worship of the painted corpse of the Lady by the Tyrant after she has destroyed herself rather than be raped by him. This allegory is strengthened by the contrast of the Lady of the main plot and the Wife of the subplot.

The Wife, sister of the Lady, neglected and mistrusted by her husband who has no cause for his mistrust beyond his need to test her faithfulness, is left unprotected from deliberate temptation, seduction, and her own destruction. Read allegorically, *The Second Maiden's Tragedy* warns that the fate of a land threatened with rape by tyranny and unable to consummate her plighted troth with the rightful ruler, a true "son of Jove," and the fate of a land neglected and deliberately subjected to compensating temptations are the same fate: death of the land. The indications of censorship in the manuscript of this play and the fact that it did not reach print until the present century support this reading of the play. Whether or not Massinger had a hand in this tragedy is not so important as the fact that he, later in *The Duke of Milan,* not only re-created a similar triangle, but also dramatized an unwise ruler who clung to the painted corpse of a chaste and faithful lady destroyed by his own hand and who, like the Tyrant of this earlier play, took his death from the poisoned lips of the dead lady.

The fallen and destroyed Wife in *The Second Maiden's Tragedy* serves as an alternative and/or parallel allegory to the chaste Lady who survives as only a painted corpse when threatened by the rape of tyranny. These parallel allegories suggest that the land will either be bewhored and then destroyed or exist as only a dead and deadly image of itself when wedded to foolish or tyrannous government. In many of the plays of the period, particularly the comedies, the fallen woman, suggesting the bewhored and defiled land, serves as an alternative and/or parallel contrast to threatened or neglected noble virgins. In other plays the fallen woman is central, in contrast with her own virginal past or the chaste matron she can become through painful conversion and penance.

The Captain, for example, dramatizes the ungoverned husbandless state of the land in its central character, a rich, beautiful widow who is sensually attended by all the gallants who would enjoy her favors without assuming the governing responsibilities of marriage. This widow, like James's England, thoroughly splendid in appearance and thoroughly bewhored, longs so to be united with heroic, experienced, stalwart manhood that she tries to seduce her own father when she sees him in full military dress. The longing to turn back to union with a heroic past is comically suggested by the threat of incest and resolved by giving her father governing control over the converted widow and her foolish gallant husband.

Similar patterns and concerns are evident in many other plays of the Jacobean years, such as Dekker's *Honest Whore, I and II* (c. 1604–5), Marston's *Dutch Courtesan* (1603–4), and *Insatiate Countess* (1610). *The Captain,* in addition, is outrageously topical and protects its topicality, in part, with its own announced artificiality. In the final scene, for example, a character asks whether such a rustling up of concluding marriages would be accepted in a play in which there had been no preparation for them. Characters also invite associations with real persons in some attributes and then deny that association by other attributes. For instance, one of the leading characters, Jacomo (the name is a variation of James), has spindly legs, like the king, is a notorious woman-hater, like the king, is a hard drinker, like the king, and is homosexually attractive, as the king wished to be. In the tavern scene Jacomo so inflames the love of his host that the smitten gentleman is reluctant to return to his wife's bed. Jacomo is finally won by a heroine named *Frank!* These characteristics certainly invite an audience to associate Jacomo with

King James and the scandalous rumors of his homosexuality; at the same time Jacomo is a hard-fighting, sword-wielding soldier, totally unlike the timid, peace-loving king.

In both *The Captain* and *The Honest Man's Fortune* the extravagant, cowardly, opportunistic courtier is dramatically ridiculed. This type, as familiar as the parasites of Terence and Plautus or the popinjay that Hotspur describes to Henry IV, is an ever-present convention turned to topical service in the plays of these years. Such figures often serve to dramatize the contrast between the extravagant decadence of the court of James and the heroic nobility of the court of Elizabeth. The image of Elizabethan glory, painted with the brush of nostalgia, grew more splendid with each passing year. In addition, of course, such figures also served to satirize both James's current elegant young favorite and those attendant courtiers who clustered around, and perhaps hoped to replace, that favorite. It is a type that Massinger used early and intensified with greater villainy later.

In addition to cowardly, lecherous, opportunistic gallants, contrasted with loyal, sword-wielding friends to true nobility, *The Honest Man's Fortune* also includes other types and patterns that are recurringly familiar in both later Massinger collaborations and his independent plays. Some believe that *The Honest Man's Fortune* is the play that Massinger, Daborne, and Field were writing when they were imprisoned for debt in 1613. The play contrasts the proud tyrannical lord who reviles and abuses his noble wife until he thinks she is dead and the profligate young lord who must lose all his lands before he can recover his true nobility and be claimed as the rightful husband for a beautiful, wealthy lady who lives in the country. The play attacks the sharking practices of lawyers and merchants who repeat, on another level, the amoral opportunism of courtiers and lords. It also includes a pretty young page, Veramour, who is as loving and loyal to his master as his name suggests, but who is so pursued by the lascivious courtiers that he finally dons skirts and agrees to marry one of them. The most ardent of the lechers insists to Veramour that he must be a girl in disguise, and since so many plays have suggested that pretty pages always turn out to be girls, Veramour is persuaded that he, too, is probably a girl in disguise. The wedding proves most interesting.

Such pretty youths, like the variety of beautiful women who have more substantial roles in the Jacobean plays than they had in the Elizabethan, might well have had particular appeal for a king with a taste for effeminately beautiful men splendidly adorned. However, the youths, like the women, attractive and entertaining in their superficial appeal, have a more serious signification on the allegorical level. Indeed, after the death of Prince Henry in 1612, the infant hope of a future good that might be born of the good land well husbanded is often suggested by the names and in the portrayal of loyal pages of tender years.

It seems evident that by 1613, when his name first appears in theatrical records, Massinger had had occasion to learn, as either observer or collaborator, both the matter and the manner that satisfied his Jacobean audience. It also seems evident, from Daborne's complaint about Massinger's higher pay, that Massinger had also proven his ability to please that audience. However, since audiences must choose to come to the theater before they can be pleased or displeased by the matter on stage, and since the name of a familiar playwright provides greater appeal than that of a novice, Massinger continued as an unnamed collaborator on plays attributed to others for many more years.

In 1614, the year following the first mention of Massinger as a playwright, either very few plays were written, or very few survived by either title or text. The only play of the ten that survive for this year that anyone has suggested might be attributed in part to Massinger is *The Faithful Friends,* a play that is an intriguing one for many reasons.[5] Listed in the Stationers' Register in 1660 by Moseley as a Beaumont and Fletcher play, it does not appear in any of the seventeenth-century collections of Beaumont and Fletcher and did not become a part of their canon until Dyce included it in 1812. The omission of a play that not only attacks the absolute power of a monarch but boldly justifies tyrannicide and revolution seems to justify the assumption that Moseley recognized that there was at least one Beaumont and Fletcher play that could not serve as Cavalier propaganda.

Markings for cuts and changes in the manuscript, written in four seventeenth-century hands, indicate both censorship and revision. The play addresses issues of both the immediate period of 1614 and the early 1620s. For example, the descriptions of the elaborate wedding of the king's young favorite would have been particularly topical either in 1614, following the wedding of the earl of Somerset to Lady Essex in December, 1613, or in 1620/21 following the wedding of the duke of Buckingham to Katherine Manners, daughter of the earl of Rutland, in May 1620. The elaborately staged banquet with its attendant masque would also have been an accurate reflection of James's court in either period.

Both the matter of *The Faithful Friends* and the manner of presentation provide exaggerated illustrations of the concerns of those moments and the methods of addressing those concerns in the theater. Familiar contemporary concerns and personalities are suggested and denied, celebrated and satirized, provocatively presented and comically protected. In order to understand many of the central allusions and methods of seeing those allusions with Jacobean eyes it is necessary to review the events that led up to and resulted from the Somerset marriage, for those events are not only central to the period, but also remained an actuality that served as an emblem of the corruption that threatened the basic health of the nation.

Robert Carr's meteoric rise from insignificant squire to earl of Somerset, second in power only to the king, threatened the most traditional and deeply venerated values in the nation. Carr's was a rise that owed all to his youthful beauty and a fortunate fall in the tiltyard before the eyes of a sympathetic and soon adoring king; a rise that owed nothing to birth, education, or achievement; and a rise that was to be extravagantly duplicated by Buckingham only a few years later. In addition to serving as an example of the royal disregard for either birth or merit, Somerset came to illustrate a royally protected disregard of private as well as public virtue.

By 1610, the third year of Carr's reign as the king's favorite, the young earl of Essex returned from abroad to consummate his marriage with Frances Howard only to find that his child bride had grown up to become a court beauty whose name was amorously linked with both the young Prince of Wales and Robert Carr. For the next three years both the king and the Howard family encouraged the love affair between Lady Essex and Carr, and only her frustrated husband and Carr's friend Sir Thomas Overbury, who warned the simple Carr that he would be helpless in the hands of the powerful Howard family, posed any objections.

Overriding the objections of churchmen and legal counsel, King James insisted that Lady Essex must be declared free to marry his favorite. Therefore, Frances Howard Essex was examined by duly appointed matrons, declared a virgin, and granted a nullity of her marriage on the grounds that her husband was impotent with her alone. Carr, with a smiling duplicity equal to Iago's, managed to have his friend Overbury committed to the Tower where he died in September 1613. Carr became the earl of Somerset in November and married the former Lady Essex in a December wedding of heretofore unrivaled splendor.

Three years later, in the fall of 1616, after the young, beautiful George Villiers, later the duke of Buckingham, had already become a gentleman of the royal bedchamber, the entire nation was shocked when Somerset and his wife were convicted of the murder of Sir Thomas Overbury, poisoned by an arsenic enema after several more conventional methods of poisoning had failed. That the king had raised such a man as Somerset to great power, complied in and winked at the humiliation of the young earl of Essex, and then saved the lives of the guilty pair when all those at their command in the murder were executed sent shock waves through the nation that were to be felt for years to come and remembered even longer.[6]

Friendship, chastity, honor, merit, service, birth, faith, and law had all been subverted with the active support of the Crown itself. These are precisely the issues of *The Faithful Friends* and many other plays of the period, and they were issues even before it was known that Overbury had been murdered, when all that was known was that the dear friend of the great favorite had gone to the Tower and died there because he objected to his friend's marriage.

Under the superficial protection of a story set in classical Rome, both the evils of government by favoritism and the plight of the young heirs to the old nobility are dramatized, particularly in the portrait of Tullius who simultaneously suggests both favorites like Somerset and betrayed young lords like Essex. As the king's fawned-upon favorite, despised by the older servants of the state, given power beyond any claim to experience or merit, married by the king to the most celebrated beauty in the realm, Tullius is a type of Somerset. In his honor, his birth that made him one of the old nobility who had proven their service to the nation, in the enforced delay of the consummation of his marriage, in the threat to himself and his deepest honor posed by the king himself, Tullius is a type of the earl of Essex. And, to many, the royally condoned humiliation of the earl of Essex was a humiliation of all the old nobility and a rejection of their past service.

These two types, conflated in the single character of Tullius, are also suggested and reinforced by a variety of parallel portraits and situations. The vain foppery and foolish courtship of Sir Pergamus, for example, ridicules the pretensions of new men like Somerset who have nothing to offer a wife except wealth that can be used as protection or power. The dramatized friendships, threatened by or subject to treachery, not only recall Somerset and Overbury, but also the larger questions of the role of the friends of king and kingdom in the fate of a nation. The weakening of the nation and the strengthening of its enemies that result from the neglect of long-proven private and public virtues are dramatized in *The Faithful Friends* by the internal strife, threats to the life of the king, and gifts of power to an old and threatening enemy.

On an allegorical level the chaste, beautiful Philadelphia, unable to consummate her marriage with her true husband and threatened with rape by the king himself, seems to be a clear representation of a nation threatened by tyranny. In addition, Lelia, disguised as the page Janus, in almost supernatural service to both her brother and her beloved, makes a double suggestion that becomes something of a convention in the plays of subsequent years: first, the service of the young woman in disguise suggests that the land itself will support those in true service, those who should be true husbands to the land, and, second, that when the ostensible husband of the land is weak or effeminate, then the wife, or land, must put on the armor of a man, like Britomart in search of her destined mate; the land must secretly husband itself and serve and protect those who should be its rightful governors.

Recurring Patterns in Collaborations, 1616–1621

The plays Massinger shared in after 1616, and indeed most of the extant plays of the period, not only seem to allude to the shocking events of the Overbury murder but also to include increasingly dark scenes of terror and forboding as the events of the decade beyond the immediate corruption of the court of King James became ever more threatening to the honor, values, and safety of the nation.

In the two years following *The Faithful Friends*, 1615–1616, there are no plays attributed even in part to Massinger. However, it is hazardous to assume that he was inactive in the theater during that time because theatrical records are incomplete and the dates assigned to known plays and titles in most instances cannot be narrowed to a specific year. However, in the five years between 1616 and 1621, the year in which Massinger emerges as an independent playwright, fourteen plays are attributed in whole or in part to him.

Three of the fourteen plays associated with Massinger for this period exist only as titles of lost works: *The Jeweller of Amsterdam*, tragedy (1616–1619); *Antonio and Vallia*, comedy (c. 1613–1640); *Philenzo and Hypollita*, tragicomedy (c. 1613–1640). The last two titles are attributed to Massinger alone. Eight plays, it is generally assumed, are the combined work of John Fletcher and Massinger. These include *The Queen of Corinth*, tragicomedy (1616–1619); *The Knight of Malta*, tragicomedy (1616–1619); *Rollo, The Bloody Brother*, tragedy (1616–1624); *The Little French Lawyer*, comedy (1619–1623); *The Laws of Candy*, tragicomedy (1619–1623); *The Custom of the Country*, comedy (1619–1623); *The False One*, tragedy (1619–1623); and *Sir John van Olden Barnavelt*, tragedy (1619).

Three plays of this period are attributed to Massinger and collaborators other than Fletcher: *The Old Law*, comedy (c. 1615–1618), with Thomas Middleton and William Rowley; *The Fatal Dowry*, tragedy (1616–1619), with Nathan Field; and *The Virgin Martyr*, tragedy (1620), with Thomas Dekker. Few accept Massinger's share in *The Old Law;* all accept his share in *The Virgin Martyr*, although it is generally included in the Dekker canon. In most instances *The Fatal Dowry* is treated as the initial play in the Massinger canon.

Massinger, exercising the methods and exploring the forms that were to shape his independent plays, seized upon and exploited the heady theatrical fare of the Overbury trial of 1616. All of the plays of these final rich years of Massinger's apprenticeship combine allegorical morality structures and surface associations with this representative national scandal. The trial of Somerset, his wife, and their accomplices for the murder of Thomas Overbury brought to light events more sensational than any dreamed of even in the Jacobean theater. The shocked London public of 1616 learned of multiple attempts at and bizarre forms of poisoning, of conjuring doctors working spells and providing potions, of secret arrangements for the clandestine adulterous meetings of Lady Essex and Somerset before their marriage. The shocked and shamed London public then witnessed the execution of all the lowborn, unprotected accessories to the Overbury murder while those who set the murder in motion were granted royal pardon.

The art of the theater lost little time in imitating the life revealed in the trial. The cooks in *Rollo, the Bloody Brother*, like the servants employed to poison Overbury, poison everything that is served to the ill-fated Otto. The servants are executed for their failed efforts while Rollo and his favorite who plan the murder go free. The favorite, Latorch, like Lady Somerset, believes in and seeks the conjuring aid of a group of rogues who claim to have occult powers. The dark villainy of a woman driven to treachery and poisoning by her lust for one of equal villainy is dramatized in the attachment of the literally black Zanthia for the evil Mountferrat in *The Knight of Malta*. This pair of villains escape execution and are, like the Somersets, married and sentenced to exile. The scheming servant and his spell-working, brothel-keeping wife who work the evil will of a noblewoman in *The Custom of the Country* receive a sentence that seems more just than the execution of similar figures in the Overbury case; in the play these accessories to crime, forced to evil by penury rather than by murderous intent, go free and receive a living that will liberate them from subjection to the dark designs of others.

In the three plays that bear Massinger's name, *The Old Law*, *The Fatal Dowry*, and *The Virgin Martyr*, there is no reference to poisoning, the occult, or the execution of accessories in place of protected, privileged plotters, but both *The Old Law* and *The Fatal Dowry* focus directly on adultery countenanced by those who should prevent it, the humiliation and destruction of a legitimate mate, and the distortion of the law that encourages such corruption. Even *The Virgin Martyr*, the play furthest in time from the events of 1616, includes a proud noblewoman who is allowed to choose one beneath herself instead of one equal in birth and rank, a choice that not only contributes to the tragic action of the play, but one that is finally revoked.

In *The Old Law* wanton wives are encouraged to entertain suitors and select new husbands while the old ones yet live by the "old law" of that play's title, a law that insists that men be put to death at fourscore years and women at threescore. A young woman marries an old man for his wealth and then subjects him to the humiliation of competition with her younger suitors waiting, not inactively, for the law to take effect. The subversion of the law for lechery is also dramatized by the clown of the play who arranges to bury an old wife and marry a young new one on the same day by bribing a lawyer to change the birth records of the former. The old wife's claim that she is pregnant, a false claim supported only by a cushion, may well be a comic glance at Lady Essex's claim to virginity, which many people assumed was supported by the substitution of a virgin dressed like Lady Essex for the examination.

The triangle of *The Fatal Dowry* recalls the central figures and issues of the Somerset scandal, invites comparison with other events of 1618, and dramatizes tragic consequences that go beyond the immediate reach of the law. The figures of the triangle are the noble Charalois, son of a brave, long-serving soldier whose service is completely forgotten by an ungrateful money-worshipping nation; Beaumelle, the beautiful wife of Charalois, given to him along with great wealth and power by her father, unsolicited, in recognition of Charalois's adherence to and perpetuation of values and virtues too often neglected; and Nouvall Junior, son of the most powerful lawmaker of the realm, a son distinguished entirely by his modish, elegant attire, his fawning train of parasites, and his sensual amorality. Beaumelle is attended by two who represent her choices of virtue or vice: Florimell tries by words and actions to keep Beaumelle faithful to her husband, and Bellapert like the lady-in-waiting in service to Lady Essex, not only encourages adultery, but provides the trysting place. In addition, both father and husband excuse and condone the openly lascivious behavior of Beaumelle and Nouvall Junior by explaining that behavior away as mere fashion and manners.

Charalois, in his birth, marriage, virtue, and humiliation by law and wife, recalls the young Lord Essex, and, perhaps, by extension that growing body of the old nobility that increasingly voiced their discontent with the rule of King James. At the same time, Charalois in his disregard for the sound advice of his old friend suggests Somerset, and in his ingratitude to the father-in-law who had raised him so high, he suggests both Somerset's threatening the king at the time of the trial, and the endless appetite without gratitude of both Somerset and his successor, Buckingham.

Buckingham as the new, all-powerful favorite of the king is called to mind by more than the theme of ingratitude in *The Fatal Dowry*, for by 1616 Buckingham was also posing a challenge to the basic law of the land, and law is a central concern of both this play and *The Old Law*. The staunchest defender of English common law restrictions on royal absolutism, Sir Edward Coke, was replaced as Chief Justice in 1616 by Francis Bacon, the successful prosecutor of the Somerset trial, self-appointed mentor to Buckingham, and, through that favorite's help, Lord Keeper by 1617. The struggle

between Coke and Bacon, not unlike the struggle between the old
premier justice, father of Beaumelle, and the new premier justice,
father of Nouvall Junior, in *The Fatal Dowry*, was determined by
Buckingham's decision, totally supported by the king, that Coke's
daughter be married against her wishes and those of her mother to
Buckingham's slightly deranged brother. Coke's beautiful daughter,
like Beaumelle in *The Fatal Dowry*, was already enamored of another,
and although her father forcibly removed her from the sanctuary
provided by her protecting mother in order that he might be restored
to royal favor, neither Coke nor the king could force that mother,
the wealthy Lady Hatton, to provide the rich dowry coveted by the
king and Buckingham for his dim-witted brother. Such unseemly
national gossip could hardly be far from the minds of an audience
watching a play entitled *The Fatal Dowry*.

Of course the splendidly bedecked Buckingham and the host of
young gallants who emulated his rich taste in satins and lace were
called to mind by both the comedy of Nouvall's elaborate concern
with his sartorial elegance in *The Fatal Dowry* and by the assembled
young gallants of *The Old Law* who gleefully send their fathers off
to the executioner in order that legacies might be spent on the
newest fashions, vain entertainment, and licentious living. Comic,
often cowardly waterflies, young gallants given to excessive sword-
play in defense of their tender courtly honor, and royal favorites of
varying degrees of viciousness are stock elements of most of the
plays of these years. In some instances the obvious model for the
dramatic portrait seems to be Buckingham, and in others Gondomer,
the Spanish ambassador who served his own interests and those of
his nation by his skillful manipulation of the king of England.
Behind both models, however, particularly in plays that question
the efficacy of the law in the hands of a government that places
personal desires above eternal verities, lies the fear of the power of
any man, native or foreign, noble or vicious, who might gain the
exclusive ear of the king when the rule of the people was vested
solely in the hands of that single, often weak man.

However, no matter how attractive theatrical imitations of such
topical figures and situations might be, playwrights had to find a
way to get their plays past the censor before they could exploit such
attractions. Just as the censorship attendant on too specific a portrait
of any particular person is avoided in *The Fatal Dowry* by the multiple
suggestions of Charalois and the tragic ending of all involved so,

in two other plays of the group associated with Massinger, censurable material is protected by displacement. The royal favorite in *The Queen of Corinth*, for example, is a deserving conscientious advisor, singled out for preferment by a queen, not a king; her *son*, however, is a vicious, subverting, royally protected villain. The vain, seducing, conceited, swordplaying gallants of *The Little French Lawyer* and *The Custom of the Country* go through conversions that make them acceptable members of the society they threaten.

Latorch, the royal favorite of *Rollo, the Bloody Brother*, on the other hand, is one who panders to the lust of his master, helps bring the nation to the brink of destruction, and expects to assume absolute control. The equivalent characters, Gonzalo in *The Laws of Candy* and Photinus in *The False One*, are both powerful, ruthless advisors who seek to destroy and replace the heir and the ancient sovereignty of the country. Gonzalo, particularly, is suggestive of Gondomer. Just as Gondomer won James so completely to his cause that he could demand and receive the life of Raleigh in 1618, so Gonzalo in *The Laws of Candy* makes an old general who had served long and valiantly in defense of his country the target of his machinations, and reduces that noble soldier to abject poverty.

Photinus, the self-serving, destructive minister to Ptolemy, and Septimius, the opportunistic murdering parasite, in *The False One* present the full horror of the execution of Raleigh in their grisly gift of Pompey's head to the invading Caesar. Even Caesar, within the play, is horrified that Pompey, who had served and defended with loyal strength and courage and had been the tutor to the young heir to the throne, should, like Raleigh, come to such an ignoble end at the hands of those who have usurped the real power in the land.[7]

The staged analogues to the execution of Raleigh, an execution demanded by Gondomer and granted by James even in the face of Buckingham's pleas for a stay, were perhaps merely variations on that familiar emblem of the national character as a rough, plain-speaking, hardy soldier. In many of the plays of these years this figure that, as has been suggested, was conventionally familiar and enduringly popular, is often contrasted with cowardly and/or vainglorious gallants and subjected to the rejection and ingratitude of the nation he has served.

The image of the national character as a plain-dealing soldier that hazards all in defense of his king, country, and friends was in sharp contrast to the actual nation that allowed the public humiliation of the earl of Essex, son of the famous firebrand of Elizabethan years, in order that a pampered darling of the court might have his wife. The contrast of the national image and the ungrateful actuality was even more apparent in the execution of Raleigh in 1618; the last of the great Elizabethan courtiers was beheaded at the demand of a Spanish ambassador. In 1619 England encouraged the execution of its old friend, that stalwart Dutch hero, Sir John van Olden Barnavelt, who had successfully driven the Spanish from the Low Countries. The English audience admired the plain, rough, and righteous soldier on the stage, but England sent no soldiers to the aid of beleaguered Protestants under attack on the Continent.

The despicable fate of a noble soldier serves as the first motive for the action of *The Fatal Dowry*. After spending his entire life in the service of his country and using all his wealth to pay his soldiers, neglected by an ungrateful nation, the old Marshal is left to die in debtor's prison and refused burial because his creditors want to make a powder of his bones to inoculate their sons against any desire for military service. The play also includes two other characters in buff jerkins who, despite the loyal service of their swords, are belittled and reviled by the vainglorious gallants of the play.

The classical source of *The Fatal Dowry* is the twenty-fourth *controversia*, a debate on ingratitude, by Seneca the Elder, and the theme of ingratitude is contrapuntally developed in various actions of the play.[8] The law against ingratitude and the law that rewards the noblest service to the land are the laws celebrated in *The Laws of Candy*, a play that also includes a loyal soldier neglected by his nation.

Those qualities that are celebrated in a noble soldier are the only ones Cleopatra will admire in Caesar in *The False One*, and they are repeated in the rough character of Scaeva who rejects all service to sensuality. After the old tutor to the princes and their loyal honest chancellor have both been beheaded in *Rollo, the Bloody Brother*, one captain defies death to bury the chancellor, and his brother soldier turns his sword against the tyrant. Although Champernel, the old, lame, noble soldier of *The Little French Lawyer*, wins the hand of the lady, he is publicly attacked by his rejected rival, a vainglorious courtier, and reduced to tears of humiliation when he cannot rise up from the ground. Lying there in humiliation, he defiantly defends the service of all soldiers who risk their lives to provide the luxuries and protect the country for those who, in turn, ridicule and belittle them.

One of the most appealing of the bluff stage soldiers of these years is Captain Norradine, the wounded, hard-drinking, singing companion of his crew in *The Knight of Malta,* a play that contrasts true and false service in a variety of ways.

But, of course, the long-serving, appealing, successful fighting man of the people was nowhere more poignantly portrayed than in *The Tragedy of Sir John van Olden Barnavelt* that came out very shortly after Barnavelt's execution.[9] The play was forbidden by the censor, and then allowed in a revised form that ambiguously defends both Barnavelt, who was executed despite his service to his country, and Maurice, the Prince of Orange who sentenced the old hero to death.

The execution of Barnavelt was considered as not only an act of cruelty by an ungrateful nation, but a further rejection of the old values and victories of allied defenders of the Protestant faith against Spain and the Catholic League. And the fear that the gains Protestants had won and defended with blood were now to be lost through apathy, cowardice, and treacherous diplomacy haunted every level of English society. Playwrights, however, had to be most guarded in dramatizing the cause of this fear because no area was more carefully guarded by the censor.

Massinger and his collaborators seem to have employed several effective methods of dramatizing forbidden religious concerns. The ambiguity of *Barnavelt* was one method of bringing such sensitive matters to the stage. Playwrights could also use the struggle between Christianity and pagan religions as an analogy for the struggle between Protestants and Catholics. In addition, by incorporating the symbols and imagery long associated with the Church of Rome in Protestant polemics and propaganda, the dramatists could safely suggest current concerns. And allegorical structures for the fate of the nation itself served simultaneously as allegories of the faith of a nation.

The dark scenes of threatened and suffering heroines employed in the plays of Massinger's initial years in theater become progressively darker and more macabre in the second half of the decade, and the chaste heroines are often contrasted not only with fallen wanton women but also with imperious beauties who consider themselves goddesses. Such scenes, as suggested earlier, serve as allegories of the land itself threatened by destructive evil rule, and it seems logical that as those threats seemed more deadly such scenes should become darker. In addition, such chaste brides of quietness could serve equally well for the true church as the bride of Christ in opposition to that proud, painted Whore of Babylon, the Church of Rome, for these designations were commonplaces of Protestant polemics. And in the years following 1617 when all other national interests were subverted to the pursuit of the Spanish Infanta as a bride for Prince Charles I, the proud imperious beauty combined in a single dramatized image the three primary and related fears of the nation: the glittering surface of courtly extravagance that threatened to bankrupt both values and the economy of the nation; the gaining strength and boldness of the Roman Catholics; and the Spanish Infanta whose rich dowry—a "fatal dowry" to old Protestant alliances—was zealously sought by James.

The chaste heroines of almost half the plays associated with Massinger during these years are threatened with rape or are raped in scenes of macabre, extravagant horror, often staged in dark caverns or tombs. The rape of the bride intended for the Prince of Argos in *The Queen of Corinth* takes place in the caverns beneath the Temple of Vesta accompanied by weird music and taunting wild figures in disguise who try to drive her mad; the scene is repeated with the same bride disguised as her sister. The raped bride marries her rapist, the queen's son. The potential rapist in *The Custom of the Country* is also a royal ravisher, the king who insists on his right to deflower the bride who awaits him in a black-draped, funeral chamber, but who escapes his clutches only to be almost destroyed by an imperious beauty of Spain who claims the faithful husband for her own. The horror scene of macabre, disguised figures cavorting to strange music as they threaten rape is included in the comedy, *The Little French Lawyer,* as well as in *The Queen of Corinth.* Although the two terrified maidens of *The Little French Lawyer* emerge from the scene with their virtues intact, they are led to believe that all their friends and family have been killed.

The dark caverns that serve as the setting of these scenes of horror and madness are not unlike the unsealed tomb of *The Second Maiden's Tragedy* defiled by the still lustful tyrant. That scene is echoed in a ghoulish one in *The Knight of Malta* in which the tomb of the chaste and pregnant wife is broken into that the villain might rape her. And, while the repeated use of this familiar setting may suggest that the King's Men owned and made full use of a stage property that suggested a tomb or cavern, one perhaps used in revivals of *Romeo and Juliet,* it also suggests the fears and threats that seem to lie submerged beneath the glittering surface of the pleasure-loving court of James who willingly purchased peace at any price.

The full cup of horrors is brought up from the underground and fully drained in *The Virgin Martyr.* No hope in this life is offered to Dorothea, whose name means the gift of god, nor to the cruel governors who imprison her, threaten her with multiple rape, openly and viciously torture her, and finally behead her. In this blatantly allegorical tragedy that goes back to the saints' lives for matter and the morality plays for manner, the opposition of currently beleaguered Protestants and powerful victorious Catholics, the contrast of the royally protected Spanish Infanta and the defeated, unaided daughter of King James, and the corrupt destroying exploitation of the land set on by evil advisors are all vividly dramatized.

The martyrdom of early Christians by the Romans could serve as a protected means to invite analogy with the plight of those unaided Protestants under attack in Prague, France, and many other places on the Continent. James's insistence that Charles marry the Spanish princess and comply with the demands of the Roman Church attendant to such a match are sharply recalled, and the potentially tragic consequences are vividly portrayed in the insistence of the governor of Caesaria that his son bow to the wishes of the emperor's daughter and marry her despite his love for Dorothea. The governor must watch that beloved son sicken even unto death, be himself struck with the marking hand of God for trying to urge that son to rape the one he loves but is not allowed to wed, and finally see his son turn against all his father's values just before he is united in death with Dorothea.

James's refusal to come to the aid of his daughter, when she and her husband were deposed from the throne of Bohemia and driven into exile, and the nation's horror that even their own beloved Protestant princess should be sacrificed on the altar of the king's subservience to the wishes of Spain are evident in the dramatized torture and death imposed by a cruel father on his own daughters because they reject and spit on false gods and join Dorothea in her service to the true God.

Massinger and Dekker set these analogies in the old-fashioned theatrical struggle for the soul of man by a squib-throwing devil and a beautiful angel. The devil takes the form of a foreign advisor who has gained unusual power in the land and who is served by two only slightly disguised representations of gluttony and lust. The low Hircius, a whoremaster, and the equally low Spungius, a drunkard, like the rapacious spirit of luxury, run free in the land, consume all that Dorothea provides for food and charity, and accept the money of the devil's representative to become the torturers of Dorothea, who had saved them both from the gallows. The soul of Theophilus that seems so completely won to the powers of darkness in his fanatical persecution of Christians, including his own daughters, is ultimately converted through the intervention of Dorothea who sends him heavenly fruits and her own powerful and ministering angel. Neither his conversion nor his own torture and execution, however, can bring back his daughters, Dorothea, Antoninus, or the thousands of Christians everywhere destroyed; Theophilus can only free some imprisoned Christians and leave hope for a better future time.

An old morality message, an example of the past as a homily for the present, and the tragic consequences of old lessons ignored were set forth in *The Virgin Martyr* in spectacular style replete with extravagant costumes, heavenly music, and fireworks on the stage of the Red Bull in 1620. In the same year Palsgrave's Men at the Fortune revived Marlowe's equally spectacular *Doctor Faustus,* another morality treatment of old, familiar material.

Many of the other plays written or revived during these final years of Massinger's apprenticeship include similar scenes, characters, and structures, draw on similar sources, and address the same concerns as those described here. The motives of playwrights and plays never seem far from the concerns of the audience, and both those concerns and the theatrical manner of addressing them intensify in the final years of James's reign, the initial years of Massinger's mature professional career as a major playwright.

Chapter Three
The Massinger Collaborations, 1620–1625

If Massinger's emergence from the obscurity of an active, productive, but largely unrecorded apprenticeship is compared to a star coming into view, then that star must be seen against the dark and sunset sky of the final Jacobean years. The dark that blighted the reign of James made Massinger bright, for the great and overwhelming issues of those years are the vital fiber of Massinger's Jacobean plays, both those he wrote alone and those he wrote with Fletcher. This is not to suggest, however, that Massinger, alone or in collaboration, produced a unilateral, programmatic series of political dramas. From 1621 when Massinger seems to have been established as an independent playwright, as well as Fletcher's primary collaborator, until the death of both Fletcher and King James in 1625, the variety of the twenty plays attributed in part or exclusively to Massinger provides ample evidence that both he and Fletcher explored and exploited a full range of theatrical entertainment. Comedies, tragedies, and tragicomedies suffer no monotony of plot, character, wit, or wonder. Lively scenes and lovely maidens, spectacle and satire, fantastic rescues and dark destruction provided entertaining respite from reality for a wide range of theatergoers.

And yet at the same time, as a part of that entertainment, the plays that Massinger wrote with Fletcher during these years obliquely addressed the central issues of the time; the subtext was there for those who chose to read it, or for those who considered it a necessary part of any stage entertainment.

The plays Massinger wrote alone during these same years address the issues of the age and the concerns of the playgoers more openly, more directly, more defiantly. Indeed, it seems probable that Massinger's greatest appeal may have been to those who were in greatest opposition to the policies and practices of king and court and that Massinger's methods and matter were determined by his success with that audience. Massinger's audience seemed to share a dream of the ancient rights and privileges of Englishmen and a taste for the multilevel dramas of earlier playwrights who had given dramatic form to that dream. The problems that haunted the imagination of the nation made Massinger's reputation, for those problems as they were perceived in the final years of the reign of James are the central stuff of drama in all ages.

Despite the scandals of the court, the execution of Raleigh, and the growing fears of the nation, King James might have gone to his grave with a happier reputation if he, like Queen Anne, had died in 1619.[1] Queen Anne's death in March of that year and the ensuing outbreak of the plague that followed her death kept the theaters closed until August 1619. The official period of mourning, however, seems to have ended with the queen's belated interment in May, for only seven days after the queen's funeral the King's Men performed Shakespeare's *Pericles* at Court.

Pericles, Ironic Prelude and Negative Paradigm

The revival of Shakespeare's optimistic tragicomedy, one of the three most popular Shakespearean plays of the period, is a paradoxical prelude for the final five years of James's reign, and *Pericles* serves as an ironic or negative paradigm for many of the plays that follow this revival. The initial plays of Massinger's career as an independent playwright are vivid illustrations of a deeply different dramatic dream. The opposing paradigms of *Pericles* and the plays of Massinger provide insights about both the plays and the period in which they were written.

Pericles, written in the early years of the Jacobean reign and sharing the nostalgic use of old romantic material and old-fashioned presentation common to many of the plays of those years, includes a full configuration of the analogical and allegorical structures discussed in the previous chapter and provides a happy escape from or resolution of the threats and problems suggested by those structures. Those threats and problems are precisely the great crises that faced the weak and aging King James in the last five years of his reign.

Five great problems, all interrelated and, in part, the logical consequence of earlier policies, haunted every part of the national life from 1619 to 1625. The first was the intensified problem of absolute rule through an all-powerful favorite. Buckingham, perceived as the living emblem of extravagance, absolute power, and corruption by most of the nation, was also intimately associated with the second problem, the economic crisis of the nation.

Although the economic problems of any nation at any time stem from complex and intertwined roots, the all-too-obvious reason for the bare national treasury seemed to be the conspicuous consumption of the court, the king's profligate generosity, especially to all preferred by Buckingham, and the countenanced corruption of those protected by that great favorite. The queen herself lay unburied for two months until monies could be provided for a proper state funeral. The king's proposed solution to the financial problem created the third, equally threatening problem to a nation that feared any alliance with Spain or the Roman Church, particularly an alliance made through marriage.

James hoped to solve the problem of a bare treasury with the great dowry of the Spanish Infanta. However, James's advocacy of the marriage of Prince Charles to the Spanish Infanta was considered by most Englishmen an even greater problem than a depleted treasury. Not only would such a marriage give England into the hands of her old enemy, it would also intensify the existing struggle between Catholics and Protestants in England and on the Continent.

These first four problems—favorites, finances, royal marriage, and religion—compounded the problem of England's Princess Elizabeth and were compounded by it. When the king and queen of Bohemia, James's daughter Elizabeth and her husband, Count Frederick V, Elector Palatine, were driven from the throne of Bohemia in 1620 by the Catholic League and forced into exile even from the Palatinate in 1622, all true Englishmen heard the call to arms. Lack of money, marriage negotiations with Spain, concessions to Catholics attendant on those negotiations combined to frustrate those who longed to see England once more glorious on the battlefield, those who were appalled at a royal English daughter in flight while a royal favorite lived in extravagant luxury, and those who saw the old enemy of Rome rising in strength to obliterate all the hard-won Protestant gains of a half-century.

In the private performances at court James and his courtiers saw similar problems treated and miraculously solved in *Pericles*. The benevolent and considered rule of Pericles is in contrast to the villainous and divinely punished tyranny of Antiochus. Pericles can wisely share the rule of Tyre with his trustworthy, nonflattering favorite, Helicanus. Pericles shares his wealth with famished nations, and when he has lost all, the sea miraculously provides the necessary armor for him to wear in contest for a true and noble bride who stands in vivid contrast to the deadly, imperious, incestuous princess who is sought by all. And, of course, the gods intervene to reunite Pericles, his presumed dead wife, and his daughter after her own virtue has withstood the perils of exile, threatened murder, and threatened rape.

At court, in their performance of Shakespeare's old, romantic *Pericles,* the actors dramatized the optimistic promise of a happy, fairy-tale resolution of the great problems of the nation. Beyond the court, in their performances of new plays by Fletcher and Massinger, the actors hinted at more pessimistic outcomes to the rule of favorites, the lack of national wealth, royal courtship, threatened virtue, and a beleaguered royal daughter. And in their performances of Massinger's independent plays the actors dramatized a darker gloom.

Security in Sources and the Values of Repetition

Of course these problems, singly or in combination, are familiar in the life of nations and in written discourse, both fictional and discursive, and Massinger and Fletcher drew freely on past treatments—fictional, fabulous, and discursive—for their plots and characters. They combined French and Spanish stories, tales from Boccaccio and Bandello, and the accounts of ancient historians with matter from the *Declamations* of Quintilian or the *controversiae* of Seneca the Elder and with names and incidents from past and current histories.[2] Not only are the plays of Massinger and Fletcher deeply and conventionally derivative in their employment of classical and contemporary sources, they are also richly allusive in their repeated recall of lines, images, and incidents from their own earlier plays and the plays of their contemporaries.

Since this allusiveness is frequently characterized as the repetition of a decadent drama and is often isolated as the identifying hallmark of Massinger's art, it bears consideration, particularly in light of the concentrated attention to the combined problems of the age in the plays of the moment. Among explanations for repetition, other than decadence or conservation of creative energy, perhaps the most obvious is pleasure. Pleasure demands repetition. Consider the child who cries in glee, "Read it again!" as soon as a favorite story is completed, or consider the millions of adults who continue to delight in the repetition of formulaic soap operas, thrillers, and Gothic romances.

Many contemporary critics have correlated the decline in the long untouched popularity of Westerns with the fate of the United States in Vietnam. The course and outcome of the war in Vietnam shattered the national self-image of the invincible American defending truth and justice on the frontier, the image so often dramatized in the virtuous, invincible cowboy bringing justice to the plains. With the image shattered there was no more pleasure in what had seemed to be a never-ending repetition of the formulaic Western.

Perhaps the course of events in the last five years of the reign of James blighted the national pleasure provided by *Pericles* and plays like *Pericles* that dramatized assurance that the gods would intervene to provide a happy resolution to all national problems. Perhaps the course of events in the final years of King James created an increasing certainty that "God helps him who helps himself" and with that certainty an increased desire on the part of playgoers to see dramatic expression of a national certainty that they themselves must restore the wealth and old honor of the nation, avoid the old enemy in Rome and the Spanish beauty that served that enemy, and rescue their own princess from real and present dangers. The dramatic treatment of such sensitive national concerns had to be carefully guarded, of course, and what better protection than the repetition of blatantly familiar materials?

The Fletcher-Massinger collaborations played by the King's Men at the Globe, Blackfriars, and, on occasion, at court, particularly during the years 1621–23, interweave the issues of favorites, finances, marriage outside the realm, religion, and warfare, in more realistic and less reassuring ways than *Pericles,* intensify earlier treatments of these matters, and make every new play familiar with echoes of other plays.

The Fletcher–Massinger Plays, 1621–1625

The Island Princess.   In *The Island Princess* that played at court on 26 December 1621 and again on 2 February 1622 the evil favorite is a foreign governor who has captured and imprisoned the king of the island. Armusia, a plain-spoken soldier, leaves the island court in disgust at the endless consideration and rejection of various plans for rescuing the king and takes the direct action of a gunpowder plot against the captor and forces him to lose his prisoner in order to rescue his treasure. The evil favorite then returns to the island disguised as a priest of their pagan religion and gains such complete control over the king that he agrees to the execution of Armusia who had been his liberating benefactor. The island princess, herself a pagan who willingly serves the evil will of the false priest and one all too enamored of the false popinjays who wear swords only as ornaments, finally longs to share the faith that sustains Armusia, converts to Christianity, and becomes his bride when the former contenders for her hand join together to defeat the plot against her country.

The topical political implications of this dramatic treatment of a foreign favorite, more like Gondomer than Buckingham (who is perhaps glanced at in the proud courtiers who are so helpless in the face of danger), a desirable bride of another religion, and threats to a king, his daughter, and his island kingdom are, perhaps, protectively displaced or offset by the melodramatic action in an exotic location, the spectacular pageantry of the king's homecoming, and the bawdy interchanges of the citizen fire fighters.

The Double Marriage. Unlike the comedic *Island Princess,* that seemingly supports the proposed royal marriage of the prince and the Spanish Infanta on the condition that she embrace the true religion and join with active English Protestants in the rescue of Elizabeth and Frederick, the avowedly tragic *The Double Marriage,* dated between 1619 and 1623, seems completely unconcerned with the topical issue suggested by its title. The central issues of the play are the tyranny and corruption sponsored by evil favorites.

The Double Marriage represents favorites in three guises. The first and most central is an extravagant, lecherous, plotting Machiavellian who systematically robs and destroys all who stand for or defend the true honor of the old nobility, who, in turn, are finally driven to rebel against such tyranny.

In direct contrast is the ruler's young relative, a tender youth named Ascanio who has been kidnapped and is rescued by one of the persecuted noblemen. "Ascanio," a name that recurs frequently in the plays of these years, seems to hark back to the *Aeneid* and to recall the young son of Aeneas, the son destined to reclaim the throne of conquered Troy.[3] "Ascanio" would have conjured a dream of a destined ruler as dear as the return of King Arthur to an audience accustomed to thinking in mythological metaphors of England as the new Troy.

The third "favorite" is Castrucchio, a foolish parody of the Machiavellian villain. When Castrucchio is allowed to play "king for a day" for the amusement of the king and court, he exaggerates both the extravagance and lechery of the evil favorite and the impotence of a king controlled by such a favorite.

In the central plot indicated by the title of this tragedy, a nobleman is obliged, by gratitude for his life, to put aside his virtuous, well-loved wife and marry the martial maid who saved his life. The story is drawn in part from Pyott's 1596 translation of *The Orator*. Both the theme of gratitude and a classical source for the treatment of that theme are shared by *The Fatal Dowry*, the play Massinger and Field wrote for the King's Men before Field's death in 1620. Many have commented on the similarity of the gathering of conspirators and the encouragement of a noble wife in the opening scene of *The Double Marriage* and the orchard scene in the beginning of the second act of *Julius Caesar*. Many have also remarked on the similarity of Castrucchio and Cervantes's Sancho.

The play, relying on and recalling familiar materials, is, in turn, echoed in *The Sea Voyage*, licensed 22 June 1622, that includes similar sea scenes and, like *The Double Marriage*, gives explicit voice to the contention that a people have the right to resist a ruler when that ruler becomes a tyrant or requires obedience to an evil law or command. The exotic setting and sensational scenes of the two plays, along with their reliance on familiar repeated fictions and forms served as effective protection; in the same year at Oxford a sermon preached on the rights of resistance to a ruler was burnt and the doctrine condemned by the University.[4]

The Sea Voyage. Of the four Fletcher-Massinger collaborations of 1622, the year Coke, Pym, and Selden were imprisoned for their opposition to James and Buckingham and the year that saw the final defeat of Frederick in the Palatinate, only *The Sea Voyage* does not include any reference to a royal favorite, although it does make would-be cannibals of those courtiers who value their clothes and appetites beyond their lives. It dramatizes the desperate plight of those who would hazard all for treasure gained at the expense of true virtue.

The Sea Voyage, like *The Double Marriage,* also dramatizes the desperate plight of wives and daughters made victims of corrupt or tyrannous rule. In *The Double Marriage* the virtuous wife, who like Spenser's Gloriana serves as the emblem of the deepest values of the nation, is broken on the rack, and the exiled daughter, a martial maid like Spenser's Britomart, is bewhored by the evil favorite and killed by her father. In *The Sea Voyage* one daughter is held captive by desperate men, and the other women, separated from all who should protect them, have created their own Amazon-like island kingdom, that, as Dryden notes, is like that of *The Tempest* without "Shakespear's *Magick*."[5] The literal reading of the phrase is appropriate, for in the Fletcher-Massinger play families are reunited and new unions made only through resort to arms and hard-won reason without any assistance from magic or the gods.

    The Prophetess.   Indeed, only one of the Fletcher-Massinger plays of this period employs any of the supernatural trappings so often associated with Jacobean drama. *The Prophetess,* licensed 14 May 1622, allows its central sibyl to stage all the fantastic spectacle anyone could wish: dragon-drawn chariots in the clouds; miraculous mind control; battles frozen in a cloud of smoke. Yet few plays of the period address the central concerns of the moment more vividly than this fantastic treatment of the "tragical history" of Diocletian.

    The full range of the hazard of favorites is represented by Aper, evil favorite of the ruler at the beginning of the play, and Geta, who rises to power with Diocletian. The imperial favorite, Aper, having actually killed the emperor, rules in his name and maintains control by carrying with him the corpse of the emperor in a closed litter and allowing all to believe that the ruler cannot face the sunlight because his eyes are too weakened by the diseases of his degeneracy. Once Aper is eliminated, the clown Geta moves through the various offensive roles of a favorite and favorite's favorite: first he is a common climber; then one who exploits the financial possibilities of royal favor; he then becomes a sadistic magistrate who exploits the power of his position for his own cruel pleasure; and finally, faced with war, he proves to be a cowardly new nobleman who wears a sword only as an ornament. By the end of the play Geta is again a commoner who has learned the true path of virtue.

    In conjunction with this treatment of one ruler destroyed by a favorite and a subsequent ruler allowing a similar pattern to develop, the interrelated issues of marriage, true faith, and rescue of a daughter are all dramatized. Diocletian, brought to power and protected by the Prophetess, repeatedly breaks his promise to her. Instead of keeping his word and marrying the Prophetess's niece, a simple virtuous maid who loves him despite his bad faith, Diocletian seeks a powerful imperial bride, one who has enslaved the daughter of a king and sets all the imperial forces against her rescue.

The temptations of power and money and the plight of the poor and exploited are set forth throughout the play, which concludes with a pastoral scene of the good life of simple virtues and the threatening lightning bolt over the heads of those who would destroy those virtues. Within this fantastic and sensational dramatization of fictionalized classical history, Fletcher and Massinger have not only presented hazardous analogues to contemporary situations, but have also played out once again the allegorical triangle of a governing people torn between the simple and sustaining virtues of the good land and the proud peril of man's image of an imperial nation.

The two remaining Fletcher-Massinger plays of 1622, *The Spanish Curate*, licensed 24 October and presented at court 26 December, and *The Beggars' Bush*, presented at court 27 December, treat these same issues, with an interesting variation of emphasis. They are more comic yet sustain a more realistic framework.

The Spanish Curate. *The Spanish Curate*, like *The Double Marriage*, includes a sweet, young Ascanio who is the legitimate favorite of all in the play; like *The Prophetess*, it traces the history of the widespread greed and corruption of "favorite's favorites," those whose cupidity is protected by patrons in high places. But the title of the play calls attention to the religion of Spain, the comic plot to the corrupt practices of that religion, and the main plot focuses on the evils of a Spanish match for money that successfully tempts a nobleman to abandon his virtuous wife, the mother of his true heir, Ascanio. It is surely not merely coincidental that the tempted nobleman is named Don Henrico or that his Spanish wife is so knowledgeable about church-arranged divorces. This merry play recalls the long and painful results of the Spanish match of Henry VIII and Katherine of Aragon. Those who chose to look beyond the witty tricks and countertricks, merry gallants, and singing parishioners, might discern an oblique warning against another Spanish match. Both the text and subtext warn of the evils to king and country if Prince Charles should wed a Spanish wife.

The Beggars' Bush. There is even more rustic merriment and fairy-tale charm to gloss the serious import of *The Beggars' Bush*. Set in the Protestant stronghold of the Low Countries, the true nobility of the fictional realm, forced into penurious exile by a usurping favorite, survive by disguising themselves and joining a band of beggars. The all-powerful favorite continues to prey on the lives of the true, exiled nobility through the service of his own favorites, who will carry out any evil deed for reward, and the service of those true courtiers who do not realize that they are being used for evil purposes and will be destroyed when they are no longer useful.

In addition to suggesting the plight of Elizabeth and Frederick on the Continent and the analogous plight of those in England who were powerless in their opposition to Buckingham and Gondomer, *The Beggars' Bush* focuses sharply and persistently on the role of money in the perils of those who would restore right rule in the face of a programmatic spread of tyranny. The true heir almost loses his destined bride, given to the protection of merchants in order that the tyrant may claim her for his own, because those to whom the heir had been so generous in the past will not loan him money. The money that saves the heir comes from the beggars, both the true nobility of his own land and the outcast commoners. The tricks used by the beggars to filch money from their unsuspecting gulls serve as a parody of the tricks used by the tyrant to acquire and exploit the wealth of the land.

The subsequent Massinger-Fletcher collaborations are more oblique in their relationship to current issues and/or more problematic.

The Lovers' Progress.   It is assumed that *The Wandering Lovers,* licensed 6 December 1623 and presented at court 1 January 1623/ 24, was an early version of *The Lovers' Progress,* printed in the Beaumont and Fletcher folio with a prologue that indicates that the play had been revised. The all-powerful favorite is not in the text as it has come down, but serves as a controlling factor in the action of the play; the hero is under a royal sentence of death for having accidentally killed the king's particular favorite. The comic Malford, a cowardly, preening, foolish courtier may be a comic glance at the type. However, the emphasis on the platonic love between the hero and his former mistress suggests that the play in revised form is more Caroline than Jacobean.

Love's Cure, or The Martial Maid.   Both *Love's Cure, or The Martial Maid* and *The Elder Brother* are assumed to have been written at least in part by Fletcher in the year before his death (even though there is no record of either play before 1634) and some assume

Massinger was his collaborator; others believe Massinger completed these plays left unfinished by Fletcher; still others believe Massinger later revised one or both plays; and some see no trace of Massinger's hand in either. Both plays, in different ways, contrast weakness where there should be strength with the strength of those who are assumed to be weak. Both, written after the abandonment of the Spanish match, seem to dramatize the national concern about the plight of the deposed queen of Bohemia, a plight that continued long after the death of King James.

In *Love's Cure* the brother has been brought up as a girl and begins the play in skirts while his sister has been brought up as a soldier and is as expert with a sword as her brother is inept. This would certainly seem to be a glance at the effeminacy of the Jacobean court in contrast to the increasingly aggressive role the deposed queen of Bohemia was forced to take in managing her own defense.

Brother and sister fall in love with another brother and sister, and the course of their courtships provides parallel applications of the old morality dictum, "love cures all," to the plight of England. The martial maid (of the land that must defend itself) must effect a mighty conversion on the one she would claim as her mate (the right ruler that can make the land fertile). Her choice is a fiery swordsman who is the sworn enemy of the maid's family and all their values. He uses his sword only to protect his own false honor and is lustfully enslaved by one he had seduced into whoredom. His whore joins with the corrupt keepers of the law and the thieves in their service to drain all his wealth.

The successful struggle of the martial maid against the false values and enslaving appetite of the one she would wed is paralleled by the successful struggle of her effeminate, skirt-clad brother against his own impotent timidity when he must finally defend the virtuous maid he loves (sister of the swordsman) or stand by and watch her robbed, raped, and killed.

The Elder Brother. In *The Elder Brother* the learned and studious brother is bypassed both as heir to his father's estate and as husband for the beautiful lady in favor of his vainglorious younger brother until the elder brother learns to combine his strength of arms with his intellectual strength and rescue the lady from the vain swaggering of false gallants. The play also includes another pair of brothers of the older generation and dramatizes the false values of one generation as those values affect the next generation.

The wealthy older brother worships exclusively the image of valor; he has no regard for either wisdom or prudence. His younger brother, father of the two young heroes, is governed by his own appetite and would cuckold those who serve him to satisfy his lust and disinherit his own son to satisfy his greed for his brother's wealth and the bride's dowry.

Written in the last year of the old king's life, the play may be topically concerned with the sins of the father as those sins may affect the subsequent rule of the son. However, both *Love's Cure* and *The Elder Brother* are too problematic to sustain more than a tenuous suggestion of any relation to this historical moment in which they were written and acted.

Chapter Four

The Massinger Plays, 1621–1625

During the same five years that Massinger and Fletcher created so many of the plays that were probably considered "Fletcher plays" in their own day and are, even today, included in the Beaumont-Fletcher canon, Massinger was also creating his own body of work and establishing his reputation as an independent playwright. It seems probable that audiences of the day knew Massinger for his share in *The Fatal Dowry* and *The Virgin Martyr*, both very popular plays.[1] By 1621 Massinger seems to have written three independent plays, now lost. Although nothing is known of the reception or reputation of either *Antonio and Vallia* or *Philenzo and Hypollita, The Woman's Plot,* performed at court in 1622 and protected from publication by the King's Men in 1641, seems to have been a valuable theater property and may have contributed substantially to Massinger's reputation as an independent playwright.

A Later Play Considered: *The Maid of Honour*

Edwards and Gibson consider *The Maid of Honour* to be the first of Massinger's extant independent plays and give it precedence in their collection of Massinger's works. However, as explained earlier, there is now documentary justification for considering *The Maid of Honour* to have been performed for the first time in 1630. It is certainly easy to understand why both Edwards and Eva A. W. Bryne assign the play to a period before 1623,[2] for *The Maid of Honour* treats the central, current concerns of favorites, money, a royal match, religion, war, and the interrelation of these concerns more obviously and with fewer diversions than the Fletcher-Massinger collaborations of the same period. The play includes a king who wants to be known as a Prince of Peace, as James did; who refuses to honor his bond and come to the aid of his friend because he disapproves of the cause, just as James refused to come to the

49

aid of his son-in-law when he moved into Bohemia; who dotes on
an effeminate, lecherous advisor and, like James, panders for him.
In fact, some of the partial portraits and allusions seem so specific
that one wonders if the play could have gotten past the censor during
the reign of James and Buckingham.[3]

On the other hand, any attempt to read *The Maid of Honour* as a
doctrinaire defense of a particular belief or course of action proves
both puzzling and frustrating. If the king of Urbin represents King
James, as the play invites one to consider, then it would seem,
initially, to suggest that James, like the play king, was so besotted
with his dream of being the Prince of Peace and with his own
effeminate, lecherous favorite that he disgracefully broke his pledged
bond to support his dearest friend in battle. That "dearest friend"
would seem to be James's son-in-law, Frederick, who assumed, as
did all Protestant Europe, that James and England would fully
support his claim to the crown of Bohemia. However, since the
play goes on to dramatize and underscore the illegitimacy and jus-
tified failure of that "dearest friend," and the Knights of Malta are
glorified for successfully defending the opposing party, the besieged
queen of Siena, the play seems to suggest that the popular support
for the deposed king and queen of Bohemia was unjustified and
misplaced—that King James, no matter how unattractive, was right
in denying any assistance to his daughter and her husband.

Even if one assumes that only a mixed or disguised allegory of
sensitive topical matter could have been licensed, there are frustrating, seemingly unanswerable questions. If Aurelia, the besieged
queen of Siena, for example, is considered as a stage type of the
actual queen of Bohemia, one who should be defended by true
Knights of Malta dedicated to the defense of truth, justice, and
damsels in distress, why then is she made an overweening, imperious
beauty who falls prey to her own lust?

It was, in fact, such questions and problems that led the great
nineteenth-century scholar S. R. Gardiner to believe that the play
had been written in 1631, the year before its initial publication.[4]
Gardiner's date is amazingly close to the date of the manuscript
prologue that designates *The Maid of Honour* as a new play in 1630.
A full discussion of the play, therefore, is reserved for the next
chapter.

The Duke of Milan

Massinger's first known independent play, like so many other plays of this specific period, particularly those collaborative plays already discussed, eschews the reassuring paradigm of *Pericles* and dramatizes a disastrous resolution to problems similar to those faced by the nation. In addition, *The Duke of Milan*, in its use of both verbal echoes and dramatic motifs from familiar plays, recalls and intensifies their themes and adds grim variations.

This sensational, melodramatic tragedy, probably written for the King's Men shortly before its publication in the initial months of 1623, is, as Gibson points out, one of eight plays written before 1622 that dramatize the Herod-Mariamne story from Josephus, one of three plays that employ the name and part of the history of Sforza, duke of Milan, and one that repeats the ending of the *Second Maiden's Tragedy*.[5] In addition, as T. W. Baldwin among others has pointed out, the play is strongly reminiscent of *Othello*, Shakespeare's second most popular play of the period before the closing of the theaters.[6]

The tragedy dramatizes the history of Sforza, duke of Milan, a husband so uxorious that he instructs his overtrusted but evil advisor to kill the adored wife of the duke in the event of his death only to have that advisor, like Iago, later convince the duke of his wife's infidelity and successfully incite him to murder her. Sforza, disconsolate on learning that he has murdered one that was ever faithful, refuses to believe that his adored Marcelia is dead and dotes on her corpse. Francisco, the corrupt favorite whose motive for malice against the duke is not revealed until the final act (the duke had seduced and abandoned Francisco's sister), returns in disguise as a doctor, promises to restore Marcelia to her former health and beauty, but instead paints her dead lips with poison, and thereby causes Sforza to die by her kiss.

In addition to the popular appeal of a melodramatic plot and sensational scenes, the play includes the perennially entertaining scenes of women in battle with each other. Sforza's mother and fiery-tempered sister are both jealous of Marcelia because of her absolute power over Sforza and his lack of regard for their rank or interests. Their jealousy not only provides scenes of backbiting and name-calling and motivates their share in the plot against Marcelia, but also serves as reinforcing counterpoint to the pivotal jealousy of Sforza. The initial enjoyment of the combined attack of Sforza's power-hungry mother and his licentious, vengeful sister on Marcelia is, perhaps, attributable in part to Marcelia's overweening pride in her own virtue; one almost wishes for her downfall.

The conflicting responses evoked by Marcelia, offensively proud in her virtue, albeit a truly admirable virtue, and pitifully helpless in her isolated torment, are matched by equally conflicting responses evoked by her husband, the duke of Milan. Initially Sforza, like King James, seems so fully devoted to his own sensual satisfactions at home that he seems oblivious to the external threats to the nation until it is almost too late. The war portion of the plot, a strand that occasions Sforza's absence from Milan and supplies the motive for his leaving instructions for the execution of Marcelia, is an interesting and provocative segment. Sforza, by supporting the French king in his battle against the Spanish emperor Charles, loses the emperor's favor, and with the imminent defeat of France, at the beginning of the play, is in danger of being overrun by the vengeful conquerors.

Sforza's behavior is paradoxical. First, with the crucial battle at hand and all at hazard, he orders a full holiday celebration of Marcelia's birthday. But then, when the French are defeated and he goes before the Emperor as a defeated enemy, Sforza is noble and persuasive in his defense of having remained faithful to his friend and having served that friend even in a losing cause. Such faithfulness and honor, Sforza successfully argues, may serve as an example of his future fidelity in service to the emperor. Sforza then divides his handsome reward among the soldiers who had served so valiantly in a lost cause. The juncture between the image of the doting duke and the image of the magnificent defender of his service to a lost cause is as blatant as that between the image of his wife as a plaster saint and the image of her as unsullied virtue caught, defenseless and friendless, in a deadly web.

Such mingling of conflicting characterization, such combining in a single character of sensational artificiality and moving appeals to the heart have been described by Inga-Stina Ewbank as "the juxtaposition of emblem and 'to the life'," a frequently used Jacobean method of dramatization readily perceived and understood by Jacobean audiences. Professor Ewbank illustrates the use of this combination of signifying artificiality and familiar reality in *The Duchess of Malfi*, a tragedy that draws on some of the same sources and employs some of the same names as *The Duke of Milan*.[7]

The figures of Sforza and Marcelia, examples of disastrously inconsistent characterization by our present standards, could simultaneously appeal to the immediate sympathies of a Jacobean audience and recall the memories of traditional artificial representations of virtues and vices in timeless opposition. The echoes of other dramatic representations of similarly realized abstractions provided enriching reinforcement. For example, the abstract struggle between the cardinal virtue of love and the cardinal vice of lechery is realized in Sforza's jealousy of Marcelia and in Francisco's attempt on her chastity. This same abstract struggle is also variously realized in *Othello* and *The Second Maiden's Tragedy*. The outcome of this struggle, again, determines the eternal fate of the soul and the future of the nation.

Of course *The Duke of Milan,* like most of the plays of this period, includes topical analogies as well as emblematic allegories. Francisco, the evil favorite who has risen so rapidly from obscurity to abuse absolute power, is an image of the popular negative perception of Buckingham in both his relation to the king and in his manipulation of creatures like Graccho who emulate his corruption. The threats to and destruction of Marcelia, truly chaste and cloistered in prayer during her husband's absence, invites analogy with the plight of the queen of Bohemia and all the Continental Protestants who were left so defenseless during the negotiations for the Spanish match. Analogies are invited, but, again, specific programs of action are not suggested.

The allegorical suggestions that are intensified by associations with the Herod-Mariamne story, *Othello,* and *The Second Maiden's Tragedy* create a stark warning structured within Massinger's tragedy and invite an audience to recall the dramatized doom of both heroes and villains who have destroyed a pearl without price by loving not wisely but too well. The dramatic elements that are combined in *The Duke of Milan*—allusion to the tyranny and religious persecution of Herod, the chaste matron who becomes the worshiped painted corpse, an evil and controlling favorite, and the motivating theme of jealousy—recur again and again in many of the new plays of this period, in many of the older plays selected for revival, and in the dramatic and nondramatic literature.

Massinger brings together a sensational and melodramatic representation of an image of horror that seems to have haunted the imagination of his age and to have given form to a particular set of fears. Perhaps the representation expressed the deeply rooted fear that any people, no matter how loving and how well-meaning, make a painted corpse of their land when they turn all their energies and devotion to the pursuit of temporal, material pleasures. Perhaps this fear grew in intensity throughout the Jacobean years and demanded repeated dramatization.

The Bondman

Massinger's next extant play, *The Bondman,* licensed 3 December 1623 and entered in the Stationers' Register for publication 12 March 1624, also dramatizes the hazards of a nation given to luxury and vividly contrasts true and false nobility. Philip Herbert, earl of Montgomery, evidently saw the play when it was presented by the Lady Elizabeth's Men on 27 December 1623, for Massinger in his dedication to Herbert in the 1624 quarto writes, "When it was first Acted, your Lordships liberal suffrage taught others to allow it for currant, it hauing receaved the vndoubted stampe of your Lordships allowance."

Since Philip Herbert and his more powerful brother, William, earl of Pembroke, were opposed to the Spanish match and often leaders of the opposition to Buckingham and his policies, many critics over the years have assumed the specific political import of *The Bondman* and analyzed the topical, political allusions.[8] However, this play, like Massinger's other plays, seems to use suggestions of topical persons and events as merely one string on a thickly strung bow.

As with many of the plays that Massinger wrote with Fletcher and with *The Fatal Dowry* that he wrote with Field, Massinger took an abstract conflict from Seneca's *controversiae* as the basic skeleton of *The Bondman.* Having fleshed out this basic conflict with names, situations, and references from such familiar classical sources as Justin, Diodorus, Herodotus, and Plutarch, Massinger disguised his abstract substructure so well that Spencer, in his full study of 1932, failed to identify the basic Senecan source. The romantically trag-icomic action of *The Bondman* is well plotted and entertainingly executed. The play's enduring appeal was probably enhanced in its own day by the classical moralistic debate and allusions to topical matters.

The governing class of the island of Sicily, often assumed to be a substitute for the British Isles in political discussions of the play, are so besotted with their own luxurious pleasures that they refuse to take any action against Carthage that (like Spain at the time the play was written) is threatening to conquer all under the leadership of a new, untried admiral, Gisco, whom many see as a type of Buckingham (who assumed the English Admiralty in 1620). Timoleon, a Corinthian general who killed his own brother when that brother turned tyrant, offers to lead the combined forces of Syracuse and Corinth against Carthage. The wealthy, luxury-loving citizens of Syracuse praise the cause and offer to send their slaves to fight. Only Cleora, the heroine, offers any more than words of support; she gives all her jewels and urges all the nobility to make private contributions of their wealth and service.

When the nobility are shamed into defending their own liberty, Syracuse is left in the hands of licentious wives, cowardly would-be gallants, those disabled by age and luxury, and the exploited and mistreated slaves who serve them. Cleora, the logical leader of the homefront, has vowed to remain silent and blindfolded until the return of Leosthenes who was so certain that she would be unfaithful in his absence and so patronizing in his promise to forgive her indiscretions that she is determined to make him eat his words. When idleness and depravity lead to increased exploitation and mistreatment of the slaves, it is an easy matter for Pisander to organize and lead a slave revolt.

Pisander, a gentleman from Thebes, has come to Syracuse disguised as the slave Marullo in order to take vengeance on Leosthenes who, when a captive in Thebes, had made love to Statilia, Pisander's sister. Statilia accompanied Pisander to Sicily and now serves Cleora as the slave Timandra. Pisandra, who had sought Cleora's hand and been turned away by her brother, is in love with Cleora and provides her with honorable service and protection during the successful slave revolt.

When the nobles of the city return victorious, they find the city in the hands of their former slaves, who have fully exploited their power and wreaked much comic vengeance on those who had formerly treated them as beasts. As free men fighting for their liberty under Pisander, the slaves nobly defend their city, but when their former masters throw down their arms and take up the old whips and scorns of slave owners, the slaves again cower in obedience.

Pisander, their leader, escapes capture for a time by hiding in the closet of Cleora who is grateful for his protection and amazed at his gracious manner.

Cleora's pleas for the life of her protector are supported by the assurances of her father that all his household has been undisturbed in the riots, but to no avail. Leosthenes, certain in advance that Cleora had been ravished by the slaves, is now persuaded that she is wantonly in love with her ravisher and orders his torture and death. When Pisander, the leader of the slave rebellion, is brought to trial before Timoleon, his own nobility and cause for vengeance are established. Leosthenes begs forgiveness from Stailia and begs her to accept his hand. Pisander and Cleora are united, and Timoleon makes the slaves pledge never again to revolt and the masters swear never again to be tyrants.

The well-executed plot of a disguised noble lover protecting and winning a noble, maligned maiden combined with the bawdry of the idle rich and the comic reversal of the slaves as masters provides satisfying, uncomplicated entertainment. The topical suggestions of a nation valuing its luxury more than its liberty, of the growing power and threat of an external enemy, and of the equal internal threat of tyranny and corruption provided the excitement of currency for the original audiences. At the same time the dramatized conflict between the legitimate liberty of all men and the corruption that becomes tyranny—the dramatized necessity for men to fight evil before they are enslaved by it—gives the play a timeless relevance.

It seems most probable that *The Bondman* spoke to and for those who believed the honor and safety of the nation could be maintained only through adherence to the old established values of the nation, the ancient rights and privileges as they were represented in the old nobility, those like the Herberts and Essex who were too often subverted by new men, corrupt privileged upstarts, and the misguided use of absolute power. The chaste and faithful maiden was perhaps seen by contemporary viewers as their own beloved England, silent and blindfolded in the hands of those who swore to love of country but had no faith in that country because their hearts were plighted elsewhere.

The signifying power of the dramatized noble slave increased as the century progressed. William Cartwright's *The Royal Slave*, written at a much later moment when thoughts of actual revolt against the tyranny of absolute rule led many in the House of Lords to join forces with radical parliamentarians in the House of Commons, owes much to Massinger's *The Bondman*.[9] Massinger did not urge revolt, but warned against the course that must lead to revolt and suggested the type of action that could prevent it.

In his next play, also written for Lady Elizabeth's Men at the Phoenix, Massinger also dramatizes, in different form, the hazards attendant on the temptations to desert the service to true and noble values.

The Renegado

By 17 April 1624, when *The Renegado* was licensed for performance, any contemplation of a Spanish match was a thing of the past and Buckingham was urging full support for Elizabeth and Frederick. The final Jacobean Parliament voted money for supplying Mansfeld with twelve thousand men and for refitting the navy, and Prince Charles had agreed to yet another Catholic bride, Henrietta Maria of France.

The central character in *The Renegado* is Francisco, a Jesuit priest, and his religious guidance is pivotal to the plot. Although many have used these elements of plot and character, along with Massinger's part in *The Virgin Martyr*, to support their claim that Massinger was a crypto-Catholic who used his plays to persuade others to tolerance of his faith, it seems more likely, considering the use of religion in the plays attributed to Massinger and Fletcher, that in *The Renegado* as in *The Virgin Martyr*, Massinger dramatized a Christian-pagan conflict as an analogy for a Catholic-Protestant conflict. Beyond the specific religious implications of the play, as in Massinger's other plays, the central issue, dramatized in the main plot, reinforced in contrapuntal subplots, and given voice in the poetry, is the struggle between temporal sensual pleasures and eternal long-proven verities.

Exploiting the current interest in the Muslim world and relying on both the contemporary fictions of Cervantes and contemporary travel accounts and histories of the Turkish empire, Massinger dramatizes an account of Vitelli, a gentleman of Venice, who goes disguised as a merchant to set up shop in Tunis in order to rescue his sister, Paulina, from the sacrilegious pirate, Grimaldi—the Renegado—who has taken her to Tunis to become a member of the seraglio of Asamberg, the viceroy of that city. Paulina, although

imprisoned by Asamberg and doted on by him, is protected by an
amulet provided by Francisco, the priest whose mass in St. Mark's
had been defiled by Grimaldi. That priest, moreover, is present in
Tunis both to help Paulina and to warn her brother against the
blandishments of pagan beauties.

Such warnings are initially wasted on Vitelli, however, when he
is singled out for the lavish adoration of Donusa, the beautiful and
royally sought niece of the sultan. After having succumbed to Donusa's extravagant gifts of wealth and virgin favors, Vitelli has a
change of heart. Unfortunately, however, when he goes to renounce
her and return her gifts, he is caught in a trap set by her rejected
suitor, Mustapha, Basha of Aleppo. Vitelli is imprisoned, Donusa
is sentenced to death for having cohabited with a non-Muslim, and
Grimaldi and his men, bold and riotous in their shore leave, are
arrested for praising the Knights of Malta in their battles against
the Turks. Francisco serves as the guide and comfort for them all.

Through the plots and contrivances of Francisco, Vitelli and Donusa are allowed to marry before their execution; she is converted
and baptized as though it were a customary and necessary part of
the wedding ceremony; ropes are smuggled in with the food served
to the prisoners who then escape to freedom; and Vitelli, Donusa,
and Paulina sail away to freedom on the ship of the repentant and
reformed Grimaldi. The priest, Francisco, protects the virtue of
Paulina, returns Vitelli to a true understanding of virtue after a fall,
converts the noble pagan beauty, Donusa, brings Grimaldi through
despair and repentance to useful service, and saves all from the
destructive powers of the pagan forces.

Except for the amulet given to Paulina by Francisco, to protect
her against all assaults on her virtue, the happy resolutions of this
play are worked by the plots and actions of men themselves, particularly the plots of one man in service to his Christian faith. The
central import of The Renegado is its insistence on careful, rigorous
service in the proven path of virtue despite all the temptations of
wealth, sensual delights, and power. Unlike the often-miraculous
resolutions dramatized in the tragicomedies of the early years of
James's reign, it is men of God rather than the gods themselves
who ward off the terrible threats to virtue and life dramatized in
The Renegado.

There is, perhaps, a bleak analogical undertone; the pagan princess
is converted to become the Christian wife of Vitelli, but Paulina,

the invincible native Christian virgin, reminiscent of the Paulina of Shakespeare's *Winter's Tale*, remains single at the end of the play. The educated ruler has taken a converted wife, but the virgin of the land remains unhusbanded. The play holds out the hope that Prince Charles will make a good wife of Henrietta Maria, but little hope that he will truly "husband" England.

The use of the pitfalls or successes of mating as an analogy or allegory for the pitfalls or successes of the land and its husbanding government seems evident in all the dramatic genres of the late Jacobean years. The pleasure the audience seemed to take in the repeated use of particular associated patterns of the mating game explains the popularity of such patterns and raises questions about their signification. Massinger dramatized one of the most popular patterns of the period in a comedy that came to the stage in the fall after the spring production of *The Renegado*.

Parliament of Love

Although *The Parliament of Love* was licensed for performance 3 November 1624 for Lady Elizabeth's Men at the Phoenix, it was not published until the nineteenth century and then from a damp-damaged manuscript written in the same scribal hand that preserved Dekker's *Welsh Ambassadour*. This merry play of swordsmen on the dueling field and in the bedroom shares the counterplots of virtuous women who simultaneously defend their virtue and make laughing stocks of those gallants who consider no maiden or chaste matron beyond their legitimate, albeit illegitimate, reach. The use of a substitute bride, the conflict of friendship and sexual love, and the ploys of the virtuous wife to reclaim a roving husband, along with many repeated names of characters is shared in various combinations and variations by John Marston's *Parasitaster, or The Fawn* and *The Dutch Courtesan*, Shakespeare's *Measure for Measure*, Fletcher and Massinger's *The Little French Lawyer*, and John Webster, William Rowley, and Massinger's (?) *Cure for a Cuckold*. The popularity of the plot devices is more evident than explanations for that popularity. The framing device of a parliament of love to which ladies and courtiers can bring their complaints seems more appropriate to the middle years of the reign of Charles and Henrietta Maria, although France had a literary tradition of courts of love that dated back to the twelfth century.

Massinger's *Parliament of Love* intertwines four love plots that are all finally resolved in a parliament of love that has been established by the ruler. The first plot dramatizes the efforts of the swaggering Clarindor who, on hearing of the unassailable honour of the proud Bellisant, makes a wager with his friends that he will not only have his way with her, but will arrange for her to confess that fact to others. He begins his assault by gaining an audience through her maid, the black Calista, who is in fact Clarindor's own neglected wife Beaupre in disguise. Once in Bellisant's presence, Clarindor immediately suggests that they become lovers; Bellisant, outraged, berates him, calls her armed guards, and threatens him with death if he should seek her presence again. Undaunted, Clarindor again seeks the assistance of Calista, his wife, who tells Bellisant that he plans to come see her in disguise. Bellisant receives him, agrees to grant her favors on the promise of absolute secrecy, arranges for Beaupre (Calista) to take her place in the dark so that Clarindor, in fact, sleeps with his own wife, and then brings charges against him in the parliament of love when he breaks his vow of silence and brags of his conquest in order to win his wager.

The second conflict, that of Cleremond and Leonora, is related to the first through Montross who loves Bellisant but forgoes a private audience with her in order to satisfy his friend Cleremond's need for a second in a duel of honor. Montross does not realize that by such a sacrifice he is identifying himself as Cleremond's truest friend and, therefore, signing his own death warrant. Leonora, whose love for Cleremond changed to loathing when he suggested that they consummate their marriage before the actual wedding, commands Cleremond either to kill his best friend or never to see her again.

The other two plots revolve around the intrigues of the philandering gallants Perigot and Nouvall to have their way with the young wives of the noble Chamont and the court physician, Dinant, and the comic cures for lechery worked on those gallants by the wise husbands and their faithful wives.

In true tragicomic fashion, at the conclusion of the play Montross proves not to have been killed by Cleremond, who is, therefore, freed from his death sentence but not from his sentence to marry Leonora who forgives and accepts him. Montross and Bellisant are united, Clarindor and Beaupre are reunited, and Nouvall and Perigot are forced to wear satyr heads and declare their sins at the gates of the city.

The Unnatural Combat

Few plays could be less alike than the witty, contrived *Parliament of Love* and the grim, sensational *Unnatural Combat,* and a comparison of the two serves only to point up the range of Massinger's abilities as a playwright. If, however, one compares Shakespeare's *Pericles* as a court choice of 1619, and Massinger's *Unnatural Choice* as a play that seems to have been written in the last year of James's life and reign, one finds startling similarities and differences.

Pericles includes a tyrant in an incestuous relation with his daughter and a noble soldier and father who has lost his wife and who seeks his lost daughter and her future happiness. *Unnatural Combat* combines these two and presents a noble soldier as one who poisoned his first wife and dotes incestuously on the daughter of his second marriage. In both plays the divine fires of lightning destroy the incestuous fathers. In *Pericles* the almost divine virtue of Mariana protects her against rape and murder, and she becomes the wife of one who has learned to be a virtuous governor. In *Unnatural Combat* the equivalent virtue of the innocent Theocrine is no protection against her father's passion that thwarts her marriage to the governor's son and heir, no protection against her rape by her father's vindictive, lecherous "friend" who, having persuaded her father to give her into his custody for protection, answers his demand for her return by throwing her ravished body at her father's feet that he may view her once before she dies. In *Unnatural Combat,* like *Pericles,* the gods avenge, but unlike *Pericles,* they do not protect.

The father's friend, Montreville, is also a corrupt courtier, a type of evil court favorite who dramatizes the corrupt methods of pandering, spying, and blackmail so prevalent and so despised in the age. In addition, Montreville's motive for seizing on Theocrine goes beyond his lechery; Theocrine's mother was beloved by Montreville who hoped to make her his wife until Malefort, Theocrine's father, became so enamored of her that he poisoned his own wife and seduced his friend's mistress. Again the issue of healthy and unhealthy marriage recurs.

Along with the treatment of corrupt court favorites, marriage, the sacred vows of friendship, the basic codes of religion, and the protection of a daughter, the play also points up in light, almost comic treatment the contrast between the lavish expenditure of money for court entertainment and the penury of those who have risked their lives to defend the country. The treatment of both topical and timeless issues in *Unnatural Combat* and *Pericles* could hardly be more different.

The struggle between the forces of good and evil and the responsibility of men themselves for maintaining and protecting the good are emphasized both by the names Massinger assigned to his characters and by the sources of the material he employed in the play. The good governor and his virtuous son are named Beaufort and Beaufort Junior; the fallen father and his son, destroyed by his father's hand when he sought to avenge his mother's death, are named Malefort and Malefort Junior. The stalwart, penniless soldier—often considered a topical reference to the poorly supported military assistance finally offered to Elizabeth and Frederick in 1624– 25—is named Belgarde. The basic structure of the plot and many of the incidents are drawn from the *Minor Declamations,* attributed to Quintilian.

Those who shared the hope held out in *Pericles* in 1620 might well have come away from *The Unnatural Combat* in 1624–25 with the sad query, "Is this th' promised end?" And yet the play in its use of suggestions and allusions from other plays of that half-decade seems to gather up and intensify the dramatic warnings against the course of the nation that, like a father's incestuous destruction of his own daughter, seemed bent on destroying all hope for a fruitful future. Telfer, in his introduction to his edition of 1932, points out echoes of *A King and No King, The Laws of Candy,* and *The Tragedy of Sir John van Olden Barnavelt;* only the first of these is not considered to be at least partially the work of Massinger. The five great issues of the age, all positively resolved in *Pericles,* are treated with progressive negativity in the plays of the five years following its revival in 1619, and those negative suggestions are recalled, ingathered, and taken to full horror in *Unnatural Combat.*

A New Way to Pay Old Debts

The last of his Jacobean plays, *A New Way to Pay Old Debts,* is Massinger's most enduringly popular play and, for many, the one least characteristic of his art. Often considered a comedy of humors, or related to that genre, this play seems more closely related to Massinger's subsequent *The City Madam* than to any of his other plays, including those he wrote with Fletcher, and yet the issues of a timeless morality and the values of the old nobility, the two most characteristic features of his plays, are nowhere more in evidence than in this delightful comedy of the "come-uppance" of Sir Giles Overreach.

Although there are no records of nor references to *A New Way to Pay Old Debts* before its license for publication in 1632, it is generally concluded that this is the last of the plays that Massinger wrote for the Phoenix in 1625 before he took Fletcher's place as the main playwright for the King's Men. The provincial location of the action, the details of provincial life and concerns within the play, and the absence of any record of licensing tempt one to speculate that this play was written and performed for a provincial audience in the period following the death of King James when the London theaters were closed.

Like many of those already discussed, this play combines wonderfully entertaining theatricality, topicality, and the moral struggle of realized abstractions. Generations of leading men have found the role of Sir Giles Overreach and his malicious machinations surefire entertainment in the theater. Critics have written at length of the relation of Sir Giles Overreach and Sir Giles Mompesson, a contemporary "projector" who was considered a primary example of the oppressive, materialistic corruption of the time, corruption countenanced by the king in Buckingham and therefore countenanced in those of lesser degree who emulated him. Such corruption is synonymous with the deadly sins of envy, avarice, and gluttony, so often dramatized as realized abstractions in the old morality plays, and that tradition is recalled by names like Justice Greedy and Sir Giles Overreach. These names, with their suggestions of the deadly sins, signal the opposition to the qualities signified by the names of the sympathetic characters, Alworth, Welborne, and Lovell.

In addition to dramatizing the motives, methods, and results of unleashed, all-consuming appetite in the plot, *A New Way to Pay Old Debts* also charts the course of the slow recovery of the prodigal Welborne who had been all but consumed by his own appetites. The contrapuntal pattern and interrelation of the careless individual devotion to the luxuries of wine, women, and finery and the fully realized dedication to the power of total possession and control of all material wealth make a complex moral statement and provide a strong thematic base for the finely executed plot.

The lowborn Sir Giles, who has used the selfishness and weakness of creatures like Marrall and Justice Greedy to execute his diabolical plots of acquisition of land and wealth beyond measure, who employs broken lords and ladies as his servants, and who holds power over the laws of the land, seeks to be at least grandfather to a "little right honorable" by marriage of his daughter to Lord Lovell. Neither his extravagant attempts at pandering nor his equally extravagant bribes, however, can divert his modest and reluctant daughter from her devotion to young Alworth or persuade Lord Lovell to become son-in-low to Overreach and thereby give over to him the means to own the ancient privilege of right rule inherent in the titles of the old nobility.

Lord Lovell is assisted in foiling Overreach and in helping his page, young Alworth, marry Overreach's daughter, Margaret, by Welborne, Overreach's nephew whose prodigality had reduced him to penury and placed all his lands, and indeed his life itself, in Overreach's power. After having signed over all to his uncle and then finding no further credit to indulge his excesses nor to provide even the necessities of life, Welborne is shamed by the generous nobility of young Alworth, son of his old friend, only recently dead, and determines to do some good for him. Welborne persuades Alworth's stepmother to come out of her widowed seclusion and pretend an amorous attachment to him in order to inflame his uncle's greed for further exploitation of his nephew who will seem to be making a rich marriage.

Lady Alworth, in gratitude for help Welborne once gave her late husband, agrees to comply with Welborne's plan. Overreach rises to the bait, provides his nephew with money, returns his confiscated fine clothes, and is so confident of acquiring all Lady Alworth's lands that he offers her estate to Lord Lovell as a wedding present when he and Margaret are married. The combined plots of Lord Lovell, Welborne, and Lady Alworth allow Margaret and young Alworth to elope, reduce Overreach to raving madness, recover the land he had seized from Welborne, and persuade Welborne to go off as a soldier to rebuild a wasted life through service. With the monster of unleashed appetite locked away, the prodigal reclaimed, and the virtuous young couple united, Lord Lovell and Lady Alworth join hands and houses in marriage.

The actions of and resolutions for the signifying names provide a revealing schema of the play. "Overreaching" can acquire much and cause great misery, but that way madness lies. The "Well born" are as subject to appetite as the lowborn, and the lowborn offspring of an Overrreach can be united with and become an "All worth." The land is best served when the "All worths" are joined with the "Love alls," and "Love alls," "All worths," and "Well borns" alike honorably serve as soldiers in the defense of their country. Such a schema points up both the similarity of *A New Way to Pay Old Debts* to the old morality play and the relevance of that timeless morality message to the moment of the play's initial presentation. The play achieves a simultaneous complexity in the manner of the masters of the age, and like those masters, Massinger, too, dramatized the timeless verities that were essential to the good life of man and nation and vividly portrayed the hazards of defying those values in an age of new men devoted to selfish, temporal appetites.

Chapter Five

The Massinger Caroline Plays, 1626–1631

The period from 1625 to 1640 is no longer characterized by historians as the "high road to the Civil War," nor should it be seen as the "high road to Restoration theater," but the various, parallel, often related struggles of the Crown and the theater cost Charles his crown and crowned Davenant, Massinger's most powerful opponent, as ruler of the theater to come.

The struggle of principles, values, and methods that informed the national life of England in the decade before the Civil War is also reflected in the plays and in the history of the theater for that period. The death of King James and the assumption of the throne by Charles I in March 1625 brought no perceptible change in the government of England; Parliament gained no power, Buckingham lost none, and the rule of the monarch was absolute. The death of John Fletcher in August 1625 brought no perceptible change in the London theater; once the theaters reopened in November after the devastating plague that followed the death of King James, the King's Men relied, as they had in the past, on the drawing power of Fletcher.

In January 1626 the King's Men performed *The Fair Maid of the Inn* and in February *The Noble Gentleman,* both licensed as new plays by Fletcher. Scholars are unanimous in their assumption that both plays were left unfinished at Fletcher's death and completed by others, but are far from unanimity on who those "others" were; most agree that Massinger had some hand in *The Fair Maid of the Inn,* which seems to have been unpopular, and a few see his hand in *The Noble Gentleman,* which seems to have been a success.[1] There is no evidence that Massinger brought a new, independent play to the stage until October 1626. *The Roman Actor,* Massinger's first new play of the Caroline period, dramatizes the struggle between the state and the theater, a state that supports the drama it will not heed and a theater doomed by that support.

The Roman Actor

In the final stanza of his poem "London's Lamentable Estate," written during the fall of 1625 when London was still in the grip of plague, Massinger states the principle of divine retribution that is dramatized in the play he brought to the stage at Blackfriars in the fall of 1626:

> Make true *Vse* of this: and not applie
> to naturall *Causes*, thy *Calamitie;*
> but piously confesse, the *Plague* was sent
> from the high *Tribunall*, as a *Punishment*
> for thy so many *Sins:* but cheifest, due
> to that abhominable *Lust*, which drue
> Consuming Fire on *Sodom.* May this be
> Insculp'd in Brasse, to all *Posteritie:*
> and zealously beleeu'd; Not writt in *Sand;*
> *So may th' Almightie stay his vengefull hand.*[2]

Massinger must have felt that he had been writing in sand for his entire career, and the frustration of the dramatist's Cassandra-like impotence is set forth in *The Roman Actor.*

Paris, the Roman actor at the heart of the play, is favored and royally supported by the tyrant Diocletian, despised and distrusted by that tyrant's opportunistic counselors, lustfully desired by the tyrant's empress, and both destroyed and celebrated in death by his tyrannical patron. Not only does Massinger dramatize the fate of a virtuous actor giving life to virtuous poetry in a doomed age of a tyranny that venerates the poetry it will not heed, but within that drama Massinger also includes a series of capsule plays of the past that had not been heeded by subsequent ages any more than they are heeded by the staged audience within his play.

In his great defense of the stage before the senate that has accused the actors of libeling both the state and Caesar, Paris vividly sets forth the function of drama: to body forth the irresistible beauties of virtue that men will be persuaded to be virtuous and to set forth the deadly ugliness and pitfalls of vice that men will resist evil. Later in the play Paris's performance of a play, drawn from Horace, sets forth the ugliness of avarice but fails to persuade a miser to reform. In his portrayal of the innocent, virginal love of Iphis, Paris inflames the lust of the empress. And, in a variation of the role of

Joseph with Potiphar's wife, Paris is unable to make either understanding or mercy irresistible to Diocletian. Diocletian who has
been an audience to the play in the past orders a performance,
becomes an actor in it, and kills Paris in earnest. Massinger dramatizes both the function of drama and the timeless failure of drama
to achieve that function.

The Roman Actor reveals a tyranny that refuses to heed the warnings
of precept, reason, or performance, a tyranny that assumes the absolute powers of the gods and exercises those powers with cruelty,
greed, and lust. Within the play the tyrant and those that support
his tyranny are violently and thoroughly destroyed, but so are those
who tried to teach the hazards of tyranny. The Roman actor, after
being compromised by the state he serves, is destroyed along with
the poets, the teachers, the philosophers, and the sincere statesmen.

The Roman Actor, written for the king's own company, dramatizes
the hazards to players and poets who serve a nation that, despite
the great warning scourge of the plague, continues on the same
destructive course. The show is adored; the substance ignored or
misread. The struggle between show and substance became the
central struggle of both state and stage in the Caroline years.

The struggle, as The Roman Actor illustrates, did not begin with
the reign of Charles. So many of those who applauded the plays of
Fletcher and Massinger ignored the didactic substance of those plays
and venerated, and perhaps imitated, the artificial shadows of their
surface. The great appeal of those plays to many in their own day
was the splendid, sensational show. The increasing splendor of court
masques and of courtier performances in elegant costumes encouraged a preference, particularly at court, for those plays of the past
that afforded the greatest opportunity for visual display and fantastic,
escapist entertainment. Massinger and his fellow playwrights, who
had served arduous apprenticeships in a theater that demanded the
simultaneous complexity of multilevel show and substance, found
themselves in rivalry with their own past plays seen as nostalgic,
escapist entertainments and with the plays of new playwrights who
imitated the superficial, sensational surface of earlier plays to the
total neglect of their substance.

That share of the London audience that accepted Massinger as the
rightful successor to Fletcher, those who expected the meat of morality in the rich sauce of other staged delights, even if they did
not digest that meat, created a demand for new plays by Massinger

at both Blackfriars and the Phoenix. In 1627 Massinger's *The Judge*, now lost, was licensed for the King's Men, and his *Great Duke of Florence* was licensed for Queen Henrietta's Men. Both plays, protected for their respective companies before the closing of the theaters, seem to have been successful.

The Great Duke of Florence

The fact that *The Great Duke of Florence* was licensed for Queen Henrietta's Men at the Phoenix rather than for the King's Men has puzzled generations of scholars who have assumed that Massinger had some sort of contractual relation with the King's Men after Fletcher's death. Evidence found in recent years, however, suggests that, at least during the initial years of the reign of Charles I, the King's Men welcomed Massinger's plays but did not require that he write exclusively for them.

The Great Duke of Florence has an entertaining plot of rival courtships and intrigue, comic scenes of wit and slapstick, many allusions that could have been taken as topical, and a provocative analogical subtext.

The genial, widowed Cozimo, duke of Florence, having no heir and having vowed never to remarry, plans to make his nephew, Giovanni, his heir and to see him married to Fiorinda, the princess of Urbin. Fiorinda, however, is in love with the duke's great favorite, Lodovico Sanazarro, and Giovanni is in love with Lidia, daughter of Carolo, Giovanni's wise and noble tutor. The duke, hearing reports of Lidia and Giovanni's attachment to her, sends Sanazarro to the country with instructions to bring back an honest report of that young woman and to refrain from attempting a seduction of her. Sanazarro, impervious to the charms of the many women who pursue him, falls passionately in love with Lidia at first sight, but fearing that if he makes an accurate report, the duke will want her for himself, returns with a most unfavorable report. Sanazarro persuades Giovanni to affirm the unfavorable account of Lidia by telling him that the duke wants Lidia for himself.

When the duke becomes suspicious that both his nephew and his favorite are lying to him about Lidia and insists on going to see Lidia for himself, Sanazarro persuades Lidia and Giovanni to support the lies about her beauty by agreeing to have a foolish wench with a taste for wine pretend to be Lidia when the duke arrives. The duke discovers the plot, imprisons the two young men, and, after being seriously tempted to break his vow and claim Lidia for his own, is persuaded to allow her to marry Giovanni, and Sanazarro (who recognizes the hopelessness of his passion for Lidia) to marry Fiorinda, who has won his gratitude and devotion by saving him from the duke's wrath.

The young lovers, Giovanni and Lidia, are particularly appealing as a pair of childhood companions and equally intelligent fellow students who have grown to love each other. Calandrino, the merry servant who goes up to court with Giovanni, provides great fun in his transformation from country clown to fantastic courtier and in his return to his role as the necessary leader of the country dances. Calandrino, in the resolution of the play, claims the forgiven Petronella as his own and vows that since all those who play the fool are dead they will get a new generation of fools. Petronella, of course, provides the slapstick comedy of pretending to be Lidia at a dinner with the duke, drinking herself into hilarious stupidity, and then insisting on trying to stay upright as she joins the other servants in their dance.

In addition to many verbal references to false favorites, the hazards of rule by a favorite, new men, and vain foolish courtiers, the play dramatizes the wise and healthy life of the country gentleman who protects the chastity of his daughter, trains her along with his royal ward in the accumulated wisdom and deeply valued virtues of man, and lives quietly in debt to no man and at peace with all.

The subtext of the play seems to dramatize the ideal of a ruler, trained in the venerated values of England's old nobility, claiming as his own the chaste bride of England that cannot be claimed by either the previous ruler (who would turn her into rude, hard-drinking, boisterous sensuality) or by the rule of a favorite, no matter how useful such a one might be to the state; such a courtier belongs with the princess of Urbin in Urbino, the Italian setting for *The Book of the Courtier*.

If the sparse theatrical records for the following year are any indication, almost all the drama of that year was played out on this great stage of fools, and the high point of that drama was the assassination of Buckingham in August 1628.

Buckingham had seen a revival of Shakespeare's *Henry VIII* in April, the court had paid for ten unidentified plays over the previous Christmas season, and for the *Dumb Bawd of Venice* in April, but beyond that all that is known of London theater for the year is that a play called *The Honour of Women* was licensed for Blackfriars on 6 May 1628 and John Ford's *Lovers Melancholy* was licensed for the same theater on 24 November 1628. Moseley entered the title *The Honour of Women* in the Stationers' Register in 1653 as the alternate title to *The Spanish Viceroy* by Massinger. *The Spanish Viceroy*, as noted in chapter 1, is a lost play that the King's Men performed without license in 1624. Nothing more is known about either play.

The theater records for 1629, however, reveal a flurry of dramatic activity and provide the scenario for the first acts in a war of the theaters, or, more accurately, the war waged from within the theaters and the printing houses against those who sought to exert courtly prerogative and absolute rule over the theater. During 1629 Massinger had two plays licensed for the King's Men, *The Picture* on 8 June and the now-lost *Minerva's Sacrifice* on 3 November. *The Picture* seems to have been performed before the full outbreak of the quarrel, and since conclusions about the success of this play have been based on subsequent events, an account of the play logically precedes an account of the quarrel.

The Picture

The allegorical struggle of man torn between divine wisdom and the pursuit of honor is suggested by both the names and actions of the characters in *The Picture,* and yet the surface of this fairy-tale romance has an elegant, mannered sheen, and the comic scenes provide good fun and racy satire.

Mathias, happily married to Sophia (the text makes certain that the reader knows "Sophia" means wisdom), longs to provide her with the wealth and ornaments merited by her beauty and faithfulness, and insists on going off to earn his fortune by service in the wars despite Sophia's protests that she wants nothing more than their achieved domestic tranquillity. Mathias becomes a hero in the service of Ladislaus, the king of Hungary, and returns to the Hungarian court for his reward. At court, Ladislaus's uxoriously adored queen, Honoria (the signification of her name is obvious), is inflamed with jealousy by Mathias's absolute faith in and devotion to Sophia. Honoria plots to prove that her pride in her own absolute beauty and chastity is unmatched by seducing Mathias and by sending two notorious courtiers to seduce Sophia. Unknown to either Sophia or

Honoria, Mathias carries a magic picture of Sophia that remains flawless as long as she remains faithful, becomes yellow if she is tempted, and turns foul and black if she falls.

Sophia, waiting in melancholy anxiety for some word of her husband, unrelieved by the comic attempts of the old servant, Hilario, to raise her spirits by affecting the disguise of an ancient military messenger, at first welcomes the two courtiers, Ubaldo and Ricardo, who bring her true word that Mathias is now safely returned from the wars. Her disappointment that her husband sends rich jewels and raiment but chooses to stay away from her a moment longer than he must turns to vindictive rage when the two false courtiers tell her that Mathias has become the stallion of the court and that all the treasures he has sent are gifts from appreciative women. She determines to pay him back in kind and begins to encourage the offensive attention of the two courtiers.

Mathias, commanded to remain at court until the king and queen can accompany him to his home, coolly and firmly resists the elaborate seduction by the queen. However, when he returns to his chambers and finds that the magic picture of Sophia has begun to yellow, he suffers a complete loss of faith and returns to Honoria as an impassioned, ardent suitor.

Meanwhile, Sophia decides that Mathias's fall is no reason for her own and sets up a comic cure for the courtiers' lust, a cure that is familiar to all readers of the *Faerie Queene*. The two hot lovers are tricked into stripping, then given women's rags to wear, and forced to card and spin wool in exchange for meager portions of food until they have learned to earn their bread honestly and to live in fearful rejection of their former idle sensuality.

Back at court, the queen agrees to grant her favors to Mathias, but arranges a hiding place for her husband and his irascible old advisor that they may witness Mathias's false constancy and her own chaste victory over all men. Mathias arrives with Baptista, the artist who created the magic picture that has now reassumed its former bright beauty, and denounces Honoria as a once-splendid queen whose living picture is darkened by her own pride and lustful envy, just as Sophia's picture had been momentarily darkened by her momentary loss of right reason. Honoria is repentant, Ladislaus forgiving, and all set off together to join Sophia, who, on learning of the picture, uses her wits to put Mathias through an anxious scene of punishing rejection before the picture is burned, Baptista's magic arts abjured forever, and the couple happily reunited at the insistence of all.

The contrast of the prudent, temperate, faithfully loving life of wisdom, dramatized by Sophia, and the superficial splendor, false pride, and distorted love, dramatized by Honoria, is repeated in the contrast of those that serve them. Sophia's servants are obedient out of love; Honoria's courtiers are in service to their own lusts. Sophia's servants are deeply concerned for her well-being, but aging and left to their own meager resources. Hilario puts on military dress to reassure his mistress, but can neither be a soldier nor bring her the reassurance she longs to hear. Honoria's courtiers are disease-ridden carpet knights. Sophia, the divine wisdom of all virtue, with no support other than the loyal efforts of simple servants, defeats the corruption that lies just beneath the glittering beauty of false honor.

The title of the play points to another signifying parallel. The adoration of the surface splendor of the court of Honoria, like the reliance on a magic picture for affirmation or rejection of faith, must be destroyed. The substance, not the surface image, is essential. The picture must not replace reality.

Scholars have long assumed that *The Picture* was not a popular success because it was published the following year and companies sought to keep stage successes out of print as long as possible. This principle, however, seems to have been abandoned by both the King's Men and Queen Henrietta's Company during the complicated and still unclearly defined struggle that seems to have begun in the final months of 1629.

The Battle in Books and on Stage

Although the central concern of this study precludes a full, detailed account of the united efforts of professional dramatists, actors, and theater companies against their powerful and protected critics, some account of that struggle is necessary.[3] An understanding of the full scope of that struggle completely changes the traditional reading of Massinger's publication history and the dedications and commendatory verses prefixed to his published plays from 1629 on. The appraisal of Massinger's theatrical career and reputation is based, in the main, on a reading of such materials. Read in isolation, Massinger's dedications sound like the obsequious fawning of a poverty-stricken poet forced to write for the despised stage, and the commendatory verses often sound like the conventional flattery of a private fan club in the face of public failure. However, if these documents are read together with the theatrical records, the dedications and commendatory verses of the plays of Massinger's fellow dramatists, and the manuscript poems of the period published by Peter Beal in 1980, then Massinger, his career, and his reputation emerge in a very different light.

The struggle seems to have begun with William Davenant's decision to bypass the arduous role of theatrical apprenticeship served by Massinger and most of his fellow dramatists and to use his court connections to move at twenty-three into the position left vacant by Fletcher as main playwright for the King's Men.[4] After discovering that court connections might help him bring two plays to the stage of Blackfriars but could not make audiences like them, Davenant took to print with three plays late in 1629 or early in 1630.[5]

Davenant, in his dedication of *The Just Italian* to Lord Dorset (Lord Chamberlain to the queen), attributes the failure of that play to the "uncivil ignorance of the People . . . that came with resolution to dispraise."[6] Two commendatory poems sing Davenant's praises by resolutely shouting the dispraise of actors, other authors, and audiences. The "Wil. Hopkins," whose name appears after the first of the two poems, has not been identified; he may have been the Colonel William Hopkins who provided refuge for Charles I in 1641, or no more than a nom de plume for Davenant himself.[7]

The second poem, on the other hand, was written by the powerfully connected courtier-poet, Thomas Carew, already known for his erotic poem, "The Rapture," and soon to be made a Gentleman of the Privy Chamber. The two poems attribute the failure of Davenant's play to the prejudice of some portion of the audience against Davenant, to the coarse plebeian taste of audiences that prefer the plays at the Red Bull or the Phoenix, to plays performed by actors incapable of making sense of a line, and to the neglect by all of the "true brood of actors" who perform "tearser Beaumont, greater Johnson."[8]

Carew praises Davenant by attacking everyone else, and, on the surface, Carew's poem seems to suggest, as Bentley notes, that the benches at Blackfriars were empty and that all the rude rabble crowded the rival theaters.[9] Carew also suggests, as noted in the phrases cited above, that the glory of the King's Men had been created by courtier-poets, such as Beaumont, or poets acclaimed by the court, such as Jonson the laureate.

However, theater records suggest otherwise. Fletcher, with the assistance of Massinger rather than Beaumont, had kept the benches at Blackfriars filled for over a decade, and in the early months of 1629 Jonson's *The New Inne* had been poorly received at Blackfriars, and Brome's *The Love-Sick Maid* had played to extraordinary applause a month later in the same theater. In addition, both Ford and Massinger, who had plays on the stage at Blackfriars during 1629, also wrote successful plays for other companies. Therefore, first by indicating that the plays of Beaumont and Jonson were synonymous with the superior and neglected drama at Blackfriars and then by denigrating the fare offered at the Phoenix, Carew made a double assault on Massinger.

Massinger responded to Carew's attack in a prologue to *The Maid of Honour* delivered before a performance of that play at the Phoenix, a performance that both Carew and Davenant seem to have attended. The prologue begins with a welcome for those who came to enjoy a new play and goes on to warn those who came prepared to despise any performance on the stage of the Phoenix that neither actor nor poet will sue for favor or remain silent in the face of the printed attack. Massinger also serves notice that it takes more invention and judgment to compose a poem for the stage than to write a "score / Of Chamber Madrigalls or loose raptures" translated from Italian. [10]

Massinger's prologue drew fire from an anonymous poet (Beal suggests it was, perhaps, Davenant himself) who, unable to endure such effrontery, left the theater and fired off a long poem to Carew:

> [so] this Mechanicke play-wright crau[s] a parte
> in sacreet Poesey [&] bring[s] his flat
> dull dialogues fraught with insipid chatt
> Into the scale with thy sweete Muse, wch sings
> ditties fit only for the eares of Kings. / . . .
> But I haue read his workes, & by the bay
> That crownes Apollo, I can nothing finde
> but a wilde desert, emptie aire & winde;
> only some shreds of Seneca; rude
> Modells of vice and virtue unpursued;
> no Character entire. . . . lines forc[d], ruffe,

Botch'd & vnshap'd in fashion, Course in Stuffe.
Yet hee this spurious issue poems calls.

The anonymous attacker goes on, after a celebration of Carew's art,
to claim that Massinger has not only wronged Carew "but all /
Ingenious Gentlemen whose freedomes fall / by this his art," and
then lashes out at all who are professionally associated with the
theater:

> Shall wee yt feed ye knaues
> ffor our owne sporte & pastime bee there slaues
> That liue by vs, not dare to iudge but stand
> in awe of such a Mercenary hand?
> Yor Censure of those brawlers I dare sweare
> is seconded by euery tunefull eare
> That's not Engag'd like his. Alas, hee'le say
> hee pleads his Masters call, receiues the pay
> And salary of a hirelinge, which brings
> The oyle to grease his hinges when hee sings.

Massinger's professions as playwright—a playwright, incidentally
who had a hand in three of the plays performed at court during
1630—is characterized in a rude comparison:

> How poor a trade is there! Were it not more
> Gentile to squire some prostitutes whore
> Then bee a players Brauo?

The attack ends with praise for Carew as a poet who sings for pleasure
in contrast to one who "sweats for food."
Even from this relatively brief account of the onset of the attack
on the professional theater, it is apparent that a coterie group associated with the court was declaring its prerogative to judge and
control both the poetry of the realm and those that performed that
poetry on the public stage.
The struggle, begun and continued in manuscripts, print, and
performance, reflected the larger struggle in the realm. After first
agreeing to and then ignoring Parliament's Petition of Rights that
he had been forced to sign in 1628, Charles I dissolved Parliament
in March 1629 and did not call another for twelve years. Just as
the Crown insisted that no judgment other than the royal judgment

was to be countenanced in the realm, so the courtier-poets insisted that no judgment other than their coterie judgment was to be countenanced in the theater.

The names of many of those who sat in that final Parliament of Massinger's lifetime and the names of others who feared the loss of their ancient rights in the absolute rule and personal tyranny of the young king, appear in the prefatory pages of the unusual number of plays that came into print during 1629 and the early 1630s. Both the King's Men and Queen Henrietta's Men released their plays to print. The dedications, letters to readers, and commendatory verses that precede the plays of Massinger, Ford, Shirley, and Heywood provide a concerted, coordinated defense of their art, the actors who performed their plays, the judicious gentlemen who supported the composition and publication of their plays, and the equally judicious audiences that applauded those plays in the theater.

The "support" for which Massinger so frequently expresses his gratitude went far beyond financial assistance. Read in light of this full-scale attack on and defense of his art in the professional theater, Massinger's dedications become an understandable expression of the gratitude of the professional dramatists for both the financial assistance that made composition and publication possible and the avowed support of those patrons who did not fear to be named in opposition to the powerful support commanded by Carew and his coterie at court. Massinger, in his response to the anonymous attacker, declares that there are many honorable and classical precedents for poets' earning their bread by their pen and celebrates the wide and noble support he has received. He goes on, in a pointed attack on Davenant's methods of acquiring patronage, to contrast the classical honorable methods of the professional playwright and the less honorable methods of earning one's bread as a parasite who exchanges flattery, fawning, and licentious service for court favor.

Massinger's fellow playwrights echo key words and phrases from both the attacks and from Massinger's defense in their dedications and commendatory poems. All speak of the necessary "protection" their patrons afford their printed art. Massinger seems less fawningly obsequious in his expressed gratitude to barons, gentlemen of the Inns of Court, and other substantial gentlemen of the realm addressed in his dedications once it is recognized that he had been accused of being a prostitute forced to serve the pleasures of the players. Accused of being a mindless mercenary at the hire of common actors, Massinger used his dedications to demonstrate that the plays he sold to the acting companies also commanded the support, moral and financial, of wise and noble patrons.

Again it seems apparent that the battle between those who "sing for pleasure" and those "who write for bread" is a reflection of a greater struggle of the realm, a struggle, repeatedly dramatized on the stage, between those who produce or manage wealth and those who only consume that wealth in extravagant luxury. Not only were most of the dedications addressed to gentlemen who had little patience with the luxuriant "new men" who preyed on the wealth of the nation and spent that wealth in a waste of shame, but much of the commendatory verse, particularly that written by the dramatists themselves for each other's plays, stresses the contrast of the clear, dignified, moral poetry of their plays with the luxuriant, obfuscating, licensed, or obscene poetry of their opponents.

The playwrights insisted that the licentious appeals and gorgeous language of the "silken wits" served only sensuality; stage poetry purified the language and served the moral health of the nation. The appeal to and support by those who were actively engaged in producing or managing the real wealth of the nation were, in a sense, political statements by both playwrights and their patrons against the waterflies and predators of the court who sought to fill the power vacuum left in the wake of Buckingham's death. It is also possible that the positions taken in this battle created or exaggerated a rift between dramatic and lyric poetry, but the consideration of that possibility belongs to another study.

The playwrights' insistence on the moral function of their art vividly recalls the defense of the theater dramatized by Massinger in his *Roman Actor,* licensed and performed before the initial attack, but published very shortly after the attack. Massinger emphasizes in his dedication that the patrons who provided the sole support for the composition of the play—a great tour de force for any actor— also urged its publication. In addition, lest the reader think Massinger was ashamed of the actors that purchased and performed his play, or they of him when they had been publicly pitied for having to play other than "tearser Beaumont, greater Jonson," the printed text includes a cast list of the actors who played the specific roles and a commendation by Joseph Taylor, the actor who played Paris and who shared with John Lowin the management of the King's Men.

Assigned cast lists, exceedingly rare in the printed plays of the period, are also included in James Shirley's *The Wedding*, 1629, John Ford's *Lover's Melancholy*, 1629, and Massinger's *The Picture*, 1630.[11] Ironically, the only other cast list for this immediate period is that for *The Deserving Favorite* (1629) by Lodowick Carlell, "Gentleman of the Bowes and Groom of the King and Queen's Privy Chambers," who protests in the dedication to his play that it was never meant to come to the public theater and that it came to print without his knowledge. One wonders if the King's Men provided the printer with both the play and the cast list.

Although the theater companies risked the loss of paying customers by making valuable stage properties accessible in print, they may have gained customers who came to cheer the players, or to hoot down the play, or merely to watch the unfolding drama of the quarrel. If there were such a theater crush in the early months of 1630, it was short lived, for on 17 April 1630 the theaters were again closed because of plague and remained closed until 12 November 1630.

It was probably during this period, possibly earlier, that *The Picture* was printed. Clearly, its publication is no indication that it had failed when it opened in June the year before. In addition, Massinger in his dedication and Thomas Jay in the single commendatory poem seem to belittle the pretentious prefatory matter of Davenant's printed plays and the equally pretentious flattery of Carew's comparison of Davenant's plays with those of Beaumont and Jonson. Having already indicated his own prestigious support by dedicating *The Roman Actor* to Sir Philip Knyvet, Knight and Baronet, Sir Thomas Jay, Knight, and Thomas Bellingham and by dedicating *The Renegado* to George Harding, Baron Barkley (Berkeley), and having both those plays prefaced with a full share of commendatory verses, Massinger could afford to take the opposite tack in his quarto of *The Picture*.

Among his other reasons given in the dedication to *The Picture* for not listing the names of his "Honored and selected friends of the Noble Society of the Inner Temple," Massinger prefers to "injoy (as I haue donne) the real proofes of their friendship, then montebancke like boast their number in a Catalogue." Davenant had dedicated his unplayed tragedy *Albovine* to the earl of Somerset and had included verses by a "catalogue" of commenders: Henry Blount, Edward Hyde, Richard Clerk, Robert Ellice, William Habington,

Roger Lorte, Thomas Ellice, and H. Howard. Massinger continues the opposite tack and includes a single commendatory poem by Thomas Jay who clearly addresses Carew in the lines, "I do not heere vpon this leafe intrude / By praysing one, to wrong a multitude"; Carew had praised Davenant by denigrating all other playwrights except Jonson, and Jonson was not spared for long.[12]

Jay also seems to challenge other areas of Carew's assumptions about poetry and attacks on poets, such as his assumption that only Beaumont and Jonson are fit models or that Davenant's play bears comparison with them. Therefore, the following lines, addressed by Jay in his prefatory poem to Massinger, seem to belittle Davenant and Carew rather than to apologize for Massinger's play:

> I know you would take it for an iniury,
> (And 'tis a well becomming modesty)
> To be paraled with *Beaumont*, or to heare
> Your name by some to partiall friend writt neere
> Vnequal'd *Jonson*.

The lines seem rather to eschew the exaggerated comparison Carew had made of Davenant and these two specific poets than to convey Jay's own lukewarm appreciation of Massinger, as so many have assumed over the years.

The Picture was probably printed shortly after the initial performance of *The Maid of Honour* at the Phoenix, a performance that must have come between the publication of Davenant's *The Just Italian,* licensed for print in January 1630, and 17 April 1630 when the theaters were closed because of plague.

The Maid of Honour

Although the prologue to the *The Maid of Honour* addresses the specific issues of the quarrel, the play does not. Instead, the play harks back to previous decades and the plays of those decades to dramatize the moral conflict of virtue versus expediency, a timeless conflict that had its roots and models in the recent past and threatened to paralyze the present moment. *The Maid of Honour* invites an analogous comparison of past and present and an allegorical reading related to the English morality tradition without blatantly calling attention to characters as realized abstractions.

Camiola, the maid of honor, is justifiably compared to Queen Elizabeth, or, more accurately perhaps, to the nostalgic image of Queen Elizabeth as that image became more glowingly rosy with passing years. Despite her emblematic and exaggerated virtue, however, Camiola is saved from the insipidity of a plaster saint by her witty, racy interchanges with her lady-in-waiting and her gentle gulling of Lord Sylli. Although critics have often dismissed Lord Sylli as a pallid imitation of a Jonsonian humor character (and, thereby, have simultaneously dismissed centuries of similar characters with signifying names), the foolish knight provides great fun and pointedly parodies others in the play. The racy charm of Camiola, combined with her obvious similarity to the nostalgic image of Elizabeth, and her unexpected, startling choice at the conclusion of the play seems a clear example of the convention described earlier: Camiola is both "to the life" and emblematic.

In the beginning of the play Camiola, despite her love for Bertoldo, bastard brother of Roberto, king of Sicily, rejects his proposal because she is not his equal in rank and because he, as a Knight of Malta, has taken a vow of celibacy. Bertoldo, then, outraged at his brother who despite his sworn bond refuses to come to the aid of his friend Ferdinand, duke of Urbin, in his attack on the duchess of Siena, scouts up some untried courtiers who would be soldiers and persuades his brother to allow them to go to the service of Ferdinand in an unofficial capacity.

In Bertoldo's absence Camiola is besieged by unwanted suitors. Lord Sylli, a suit of clothes with no tag of mother wit to recognize the complete rejection of Camiola's irony, persuades himself that Camiola dotes on him. Fulgentio, the king's pampered and powerful favorite, who considers that Camiola should be flattered and grateful that he desires her poor self and rich fortune, first responds to her refusal to marry one who looks more like a woman than a man by commanding her in the king's name to marry him. When she still refuses, he threatens to smear her reputation by allowing all to believe that he has had her without benefit of clergy. Infuriated by such an insult to the adored daughter of his old master, the everfaithful Adorni challenges Fulgentio and beats him soundly only to be roundly chastised by Camiola for seeming to have a claim that sanctions him as her defender. When the king himself comes to plead Fulgentio's suit, Camiola successfully defends her ancient rights and privilege to be master of herself and reports Fulgentio's rude slanders to her reputation. The king exiles Fulgentio from her presence and his own.

Camiola does marry Bertoldo, but they do not live happily ever after. When Bertoldo and his unseasoned comrades go into battle they are quickly defeated and imprisoned by the soldiers of Gonzaga who as a Knight of Malta has come to defend a lady in distress, the threatened duchess of Siena. The young carpet knights are ransomed almost at once, but Bertoldo remains imprisoned as the slave of Gonzaga, who recognizes him as a fellow Knight of Malta and strips him of the insignia. The king, fearful of besmirching his own neutrality, seizes Bertoldo's fortune and refuses to ransom his brother. Camiola, learning of his plight, ransoms Bertoldo, weds him by proxy, and makes all her fortune available to him. When Aurelia, the duchess of Siena, sees Bertoldo, a free man in his own rich apparel, she is hopelessly smitten and offers herself and all that is hers to him. Bertoldo weighs his love for and obligation to Camiola against the luxurious beauty and crown offered by Aurelia, finds the offered crown outweighs all else, and agrees to marry Aurelia.

Aurelia and Bertoldo return to Sicily, make peace with King Roberto, and prepare to marry. Camiola stops the king in the wedding procession, presents her marriage contract, and tells her story. All are horrified at Bertoldo who falls before Camiola and begs her to take vengeance on him. All she asks is that he wish her well on this her wedding day. Paulo, her confessor, then announces that Camiola has been married to the church; she has taken vows as a nun. Camiola bequeaths her wealth to the nunnery, pious causes, and the faithful Adorni; urges Bertoldo to return to the Knights of Malta and is seconded by Gonzaga who returns his insignia; makes peace between the king and Fulgentio, but warns the king not to love his friend beyond his merits; and encourages the duke of Urbin and the duchess of Siena to make a match. Roberto declares,

> She well deserves
> Her name, the Maid of Honor! May she stand
> To all posterity, a faire example
> For noble Maides to imitate. Since to live
> In wealth and pleasure is common; but to part with
> Such poyson'd baites is rare, there being nothing

> Upon this Stage of life to be commended,
> Though well begun, till it be fully ended.
> (5.2.297–304)

If the audience had not seen Camiola as an emblem before the end of the play, this final speech must have corrected their vision.

At the same time, there is an irony in Roberto's words. If all noble maids imitate Camiola, then only ignoble maids will be left to people the nation. This irony repeats and reinforces the signification of that final emblem of Camiola as "cloistered honor." The maid of honor, so close to the venerated image of Elizabeth, is simultaneously the image of England itself cloistered, married only to faith, for no one "upon this stage of life" can seem to resist the poisonous baits of wealth and pleasure and prove a true governing husband.

The grim resolution stated in Roberto's final words is a suspended resolution; the emblem of virtue removes herself from this stage of life, and the weak king and the others, no matter how well begun, have yet to work out the ending, and it is not filled with fertile promise. The king is rejoined by a chastened Fulgentio, Bertoldo reassumes his vow of celibacy, and the duchess of Siena may settle for the duke of Urbin whom she fought a war to deny.

The unsatisfying resolution of the play is matched by the frustration of generic expectations. Camiola's ultimate decision to reject Bertoldo and to go into a convent may be a satisfying emblem, but it is in unsatisfying conflict with either the comedic or tragicomedic expectations created by the play. A long tradition of comedies and tragicomedies that dramatize the often painful education of a young hero creates the expectation that Camiola, having brought Bertoldo to a penitent realization of his failed honor and her true worth, will forgive him and the two will form an enlightened union. The play read on the level of story alone leaves expectations unfulfilled and the imagination puzzled.

Although Massinger himself considered the play a tragicomedy, it meets few of the expectations created by that designation, as Russ McDonald has pointed out.[13] Perhaps the unsatisfying resolution of the comic structure and Roberto's puzzling final words direct the audience to the tragedy outside the play on the stage of life; perhaps the play is termed tragicomic because it combines the comedy of fiction and the tragedy of reality. So much that had been well begun in England must have seemed lost to the poisonous baits of wealth and pleasure.

The play reinforces both an unpromising reflection of the age it addresses and, like *The Roman Actor*, the failure of past warnings against the poisons that continued to sicken the national soul. The primary method of reinforcement is an incremental repetition of allusions to history, earlier plays, and didactic nondramatic writings. Critics, since Mason in 1779, have agreed that *The Maid of Honour* is rich in political and historical allusions and have disagreed about the specific targets of those allusions.[14] The topical allusions are confounding because they allude, simultaneously, to recurring or ongoing patterns in the national life.

Fulgentio, for example, as many have pointed out, is an accurate portrait of Buckingham at the height of his powers over a doting, peace-loving king who did not hesitate to pander for him. And, although Buckingham had been dead for a year and a half when the play first came to the stage, his hated image and his absolute power over Charles was still vivid in the national consciousness, and, already, a host of imitators wielded power over lesser domains in the court of Charles. However, Fulgentio is also an accurate portrait of Somerset claiming the highborn wife of another with the king's sanction. In addition, he recalls the stage type of the lecherous favorite familiar from dozens of Jacobean plays, particularly those of Fletcher and Massinger. Both history and drama had warned against the hazard, but the warning remained unheeded and the maid of honor of the nation itself was still threatened by new men able to bend the royal will to the service of their appetites.

Just as the play bristles with topical associations with such compound references and signification, so it resonates with echoes from other plays of the period, as Eva A. W. Bryne in particular has pointed out.[15] And yet the combination of familiar parts add up to an unfamiliar whole. Just as the play is political but nonpartisan so it is derivative but original. Simultaneously, the play is a relentless dramatization of the problems of and threats to those eternal virtues that constitute true nobility in any age: a man's given word or promise, fidelity to justice, familial obligations, protection of the rights and chastity of others, and gratitude.

The familiar and entertaining story laced through with topical suggestions and insistent in its dramatization of moral conflicts speaks in temporal terms of timeless values. The play does not seek to give specific advice about temporal politics or foreign affairs, but it does dramatize the eternal hazards to any nation that neglects eternal values. The echoes from other plays and reiteration of familiar themes and patterns brings reinforcement to this central concern and stresses the seemingly universal belief that the path of virtue is the same for all men and all nations and that deviation from that path always brings peril. Just as the use of an old familiar story from Boccaccio through Painter serves to stress the timelessness of the values, so the echoes from other plays serve to make all those plays variations on the same timeless theme.

It is certainly possible that the sense of the writer's futility expressed by the recall of so many unheeded warnings drew on Massinger's own growing realization that the same shoddy methods of acquiring and exploiting political power that had long threatened the government of the nation were also threatening his own profession as playwright. His role as the successor of Fletcher was being threatened by Davenant who had risen in less than a decade from the penniless son of an Oxford innkeeper to one with powerful royal protection acquired by means of fine clothes bought on loan and a talent for making himself attractive and serviceable to the right people in high places. Davenant sang the praises of Carew's erotic poetry, much of which was written to assist more powerful lords in their seductions of ladies at court.[16]

Opponent Departs; Opposition Continues

Davenant, whose failed plays began the fray, was taken out of the action and off the scene early in 1630 by "a terrible clap [he got] of a Black handsome wench that lay in Axe-Yard, Westminister," according to Aubrey.[17] Syphilis and the mercury poisoning caused by the cure kept him in the country, away from London, for two years, almost cost him his life, and did cost him his nose. Massinger, perhaps, chose to remind his readers of his opponent's fate by including a poem by Danyel Lakyn, author of a treatise on syphilis, in the 1630 edition of *The Renegado*.

Although the battle had begun with Davenant, it did not end with his departure from the scene. The professional dramatists continued to address the specific issues of the nature, function, and judgment of poetry in the prefatory materials of their printed texts

throughout the 1630s. And the opposing faction continued to dis-
rupt performances at the public playhouses, and perhaps exerted
pressure behind the scenes to make life more difficult for the professional dramatists. Massinger seems to have been a particular target.
In January 1631 Herbert refused to license Massinger's *Believe as
You List* because the play dramatized the tragic history of Sebastian
of Portugal at the hands of the king of Spain and there was a sworn
peace between England and Spain. Massinger simply changed the
names of the characters, the time, and place of the action and
resubmitted the play; it was licensed for the King's Men in May
1631. In the meantime Massinger's *The Emperor of the East,* licensed
for the King's Men in March of the same year, seems to have
encountered an organized claque of opposition. The quarto includes
a prologue that seems to refer to the furor caused by Massinger's
defiant prologue to *The Maid of Honour* of the year before, a court
prologue and commendatory verse that describe a hostile reception,
and a puzzling epilogue about the youth of the actor who played
the emperor. Is it possible that Massinger had his own allies at court
who arranged for a special performance of his play before the king?
A performance with a particularly appealing boy actor playing his
first adult role? Or, perhaps, a young courtier whose heart lay with
the professional dramatists made his amateur debut in a single
performance before the king?

The events of the year suggest that one young courtier, a friend
of Massinger, might have been available for the role. In November
of that year, 1631, the newly born Princess Mary was committed
to the care of Lady Katherine Stanhope, to whom Massinger had
presented a poem as a "Newyeares Guift" and dedicated *The Duke
of Milan* in 1623. Lady Stanhope, the sister of the earl of Huntingdon
who had been Fletcher's patron, was related by marriage to Baron
Berkeley, to whom Massinger had dedicated *The Renegado* in 1630;
she was mother-in-law to Lord John Mohun, to whom Massinger
dedicated *The Emperor of the East* in 1632, and she was grandmother
of Sir Aston Cokayne, John Mohun's nephew and Massinger's devoted young friend to whom we owe our knowledge of Massinger's
share in the Beaumont and Fletcher canon. Massinger mentions
Cokayne in the dedication to *Emperor of the East,* and the young man
wrote commendatory verse for the play. Is it possible that Sir Aston
played the emperor in a special performance before the king? Was
such a performance arranged that Massinger might petition the king,

as he does in the prologue, to set his work free of the "calumnie" of some "Catos of the Stage"?

Massinger may have acquired a powerful partisan at court. Sir Philip Herbert, to whom Massinger had dedicated *The Bondman* in 1624, became fourth earl of Pembroke and Lord Chamberlain in 1630 when his elder brother died. The queen, whose most devoted courtiers, including her own Lord Chamberlain, supported the Davenant-Carew coterie, did not like Sir Philip, and he might have used his office to establish a balance of power. Perhaps Herbert arranged for *The Emperor of the East* to be presented before the king after the queen's men cried it down in the theater.

The Emperor of the East

The Emperor of the East is an odd mixture of the daily dirt of topical concerns, the allegorical suggestions of a morality play, and a child-like fairy tale. The opening scenes sketch in with bold strokes the black-and-white opposition of the Astraea-like rule of Pulcheria (the protectress until her younger brother assumes his duties as emperor) and the court parasites and self-serving attendants to the young emperor. Both Pulcheria and those self-seekers who hope to come into their own when the emperor assumes the throne place their future hopes on the beautiful, young Athenais, refugee princess from another realm.

The parasites, plague sores of the kingdom, are dramatized and described in some detail. The Informer who, like one Mr. Carleton, equerry to the king, who was fined five hundred marks in the Star Chamber in 1628 for such practice,[18] brings in offenders and seeks their conviction in order to acquire their estates. The prosperous Projector, who describes himself as a broker, imposes a price, in the name of the king, on every act of a subject's life. The Minion of the Suburbs is a pimp who destroys morals and marriages. And the Master of Manners seduces all away from sensible service and schools them in fashion and apish imitation. Pulcheria, who carefully examines all petitions and gives her full concentration to governing the kingdom, banishes all of them from the court.

Pulcheria, who is on one level all the wisdom of good rule associated with the nostalgic image of Elizabeth and on another a figure of the motherland itself with more than mortal powers to reward or punish those who serve her, sees in the friendless, pagan

princess Athenais a way to continue her control over her younger
brother once he has become emperor. Under Pulcheria's care, Athenais is adorned as the princess she is, assigned to Paulinus for
religious instruction, and presented as a possible bride to the young
Theodosius, who has now assumed his powers as emperor. When
Theodosius is so completely smitten by the first sight of Athenais
that he insists on marrying her at once, Pulcheria tells the bride-
to-be to remember who helped her to such good fortune and elicits
an expression of gratitude and a promise of obedience in all things.

Once Theodosius and Athenais are married, however, and the
uxorious young emperor is so extravagant in his adoration that he
sets prisoners free, signs all petitions presented to him, and dismisses
all concerns of state in order to spend his time with Athenais, the
empress refuses to follow Pulcheria's advice to serve as a guide and
advisor to her husband. Pulcheria, watching all her careful husbandry of the realm disappear in her brother's profligate pattern that
he calls royal magnificence, determines to curb his ways and punish
Athenais's ingratitude by taking advantage of her brother's careless
signing of all petitions.

Theodosius signs the petition Pulcheria presents to him and learns
later to his chagrin that he had given Pulcheria a deed to his wife.
When Theodosius confronts his sister, he humbly confesses how
foolishly careless he has been in his course of government and grate-
fully accepts his wife from his sister who tears up her deed and
returns Athenais. Athenais is less sanguine than her husband and
does not hide her displeasure that Pulcheria would consider herself
the equal of an empress. Pulcheria warns Athenais that pride goeth
before a fall.

And then the plot, in the fourth act of the play, turns fairy tale.
A farmer brings a prize apple to his emperor who, in turn, sends
it as a gift to Athenais, who, distraught over the illness of her old
mentor, Paulinus, sends it to Paulinus who finds the apple too fine
for any but his king and, therefore, returns it to Theodosius. Theodosius, recognizing the apple, flies into a sudden jealousy and assumes that Paulinus is not only enjoying Athenais but is boldly
taunting the cuckolded husband by demonstrating that the emper-
or's gifts are in turn given to him. When Theodosius confronts
Athenais and asks her about the apple, she lies. Theodosius sentences
Athenais to life imprisonment, Paulinus to death, and then falls

into a near-fatal melancholy that is, later, made even worse when he is offered proof that Paulinus and Athenais were innocent.

Persuaded to put his mind at ease by going to his distraught, imprisoned wife in the guise of a holy confessor and hearing her admission of guilt, Theodosius is made even more miserable by Athenais's admission that she can never forgive herself for her perjury that caused the death of the innocent Paulinus. Theodosius is forced to recognize himself as one who has ruled by passion rather than reason, one who has cruelly imprisoned and murdered the innocent.

The penitent emperor begs Philinax to confess that he disobeyed orders and allowed Paulinus to live, but Philinax swears he killed that good old man even after learning that he had been a eunuch since childhood and could not have been guilty of the crime he was charged with. Then Paulinus appears. Philinax, too, had lied, and all are happier and wiser.

With the hindsight of history, Theodosius and Athenais, whom he calls Eudoxia, seem dramatized types of Charles and Henrietta Maria,[19] and the warnings to the young emperor and empress within the play seem very much the warnings that much of the nation would have their own king and queen heed. The play includes some unexplained contradictions, some false starts that are left undeveloped or unexplained, and some peculiar implications. Athenais swears early in the play that she will never abandon her own religion, and then goes off at once with Paulinus and returns a Christian. The account of Athenais's father who on his deathbed left his daughter no dower except the prophecy that she would become greater than her brothers (who turn her out, penniless and unprotected, to find her promised greatness) seems sketched in at inordinate length but goes no further than to serve as a prophecy to Athenais's marriage to the emperor; her brothers are not mentioned again. After Athenais has been humiliated by becoming the property of Pulcheria, Chrysapius, one of the eunuchs of the emperor's chamber, suggests that if Athenais trusts him he will help her take revenge on Pulcheria, and Athenais agrees to think about it; no further mention of the incident is made.

Paulinus, an obvious emblem of right religion in his name, character, and role as holy mentor, was castrated and made impotent in his childhood. Even the title of the play must have given many pause. When Charles II was born the spring before, those who hoped

Henrietta Maria would never have a son and that the crown of
England would go to the son of Elizabeth of Bohemia expressed
their disappointment in the little verse,

> Now there is born a valiant prince in' the West
> That shall eclipse the kingdoms of the East.[20]

The title, *Emperor of the East,* may well have called this verse to
mind and created an expectation that the play related to national
dreams dashed by the birth of the new prince. However, the serious
import of the play and its allusions to actuality are outweighed by
the fairy-tale froth of the plot and its blatant artificiality. The same
can hardly be said of *Believe as You List* that came to the stage two
months later, but was not printed until the nineteenth century.

Believe as You List

Just as Pulcheria in *Emperor of the East* seems a type of that wise
rule of the past that is accessible as a model for and guide to the
present, so Antiochus in *Believe as You List* seems a type of kingship
that all remember, venerate, and serve in words but deny and destroy
in their bondage to tyranny. Considering these two plays of the
same immediate period as two sides of the same coin—one, the
happy reward of learning and following virtue; the other, the promised doom to all who deny and reject virtue—illuminates the morality subtext of both and the relation of those subtexts to the
national concerns.

Antiochus, the king of East Asia, assumed to have been dead for
twenty-two years, returns and is recognized by those who had known
him in the past. But he finds that everyone is now subservient to
Rome. From the most insignificant tradesman to the powerful king-
doms, such as Carthage, that had been his allies in the past, all
bow to Rome, dramatized in the play by the Machiavellian Flaminius.

Antiochus had fallen in a disastrous battle in an ill-advised war
and, in despair over having led so many to destruction, retired to
a hermitage where he has been instructed by Stoic philosophers who
insist after twenty-two years that he must return to the world and
resume his kingship. At the time of his defeat Rome gave out that
Antiochus had been killed and staged an elaborate funeral for him.
Over the years the rumor that Antiochus is still alive has persisted,

and several impostors have rallied a following before they were revealed and executed.

The course of the play is the tragic course of Antiochus's search for support and protection from those he had protected in the past. The bondmen he protected in his exile rob him and send him into Carthage as a beggar and then go to Flaminius to betray him for money; they are promised reward and immediately executed. The oppressed merchants and the fat priest, Berecinthius, become his underground supporters, but ultimately the merchants who are not executed inform in exchange for their pardons, and Berecinthius is starved to atheism before he is executed. Carthage, proud of its just independence and protection of freedom, recognizes Antiochus, but will not inflame Rome by being the first to affirm his identity openly and defend him. King Prusias swears a royal oath to protect Antiochus, but when the king's old tutor, promised a title by Rome, paints a grim picture of the war that will ensue if Rome is defied, Prusias breaks his oath and turns Antiochus over to Rome as a prisoner.

Flaminius, having Antiochus in his power, seeks a way to destroy the man and the image of the virtue of that man that lives in the hearts and minds of those who have not protected him. Flaminius finds that Antiochus responds to torture and deprivation with renewed constancy and greater heroism; that he resists the temptation to submit to despair and commit suicide when occasion and implements are provided; and rejects sensual temptations out of hand. Even public defilement and ridicule increase his image of majesty in the eyes of the people. In the final scene of the play Flaminius allows Antiochus's old friends, Marcellus, the proconsul of Syracuse, and his wife Cornelia, to meet Antiochus who is introduced to them condemned as an imposter. When Antiochus gives his friends irrefutable proof of his identity and they kneel in recognition, Flaminius threatens to punish them for treason. Marcellus then arrests Flaminius for bribing the merchants of Carthage. Flaminius is defeated, but nothing can save Antiochus.

Believe as You List is unrelenting in its portrayal of the self-serving expediency that subverts the most noble intentions of would-be honorable men. Herbert was wise to force Massinger to change Sebastian's name to Antiochus and the locale from Spain to Africa, even if the changes were required for other reasons; the play is more powerful and timeless without the palliative of a specific identified enemy. But one wonders how many people thought of Massinger's play a year and a half later when word came that Prince Frederick, the deposed Elector Palatinate and king of Bohemia was dead.

Massinger had yet another play licensed for the King's Men in 1631, the now-lost *Unfortunate Piety*, a title that has become more provocative since two scholars, P. G. Phialas and J. E. Gray, independently identified a story called "The Fortunate Piety" as the source of *The Emperor of the East*.[21] In 1632 three of Massinger's plays, *The Maid of Honour, The Fatal Dowry,* and *The Emperor of the East* were printed, and *The City Madam,* so often described as a Jonsonian comedy, was licensed for the King's Men. Since *The City Madam* was not printed until twenty years after Massinger's death, there is not even a dedication or set of verses to give any indication of its reception.

Jonson himself brought his *Magnetic Lady* to the stage at Black-friars in 1632 to scurrilous attack and hooting by Inigo Jones and the printer Nathaniel Butter, among others. And the Master of the Revels threatened to disallow Shirley's *The Ball* at the Phoenix because "ther were divers personated so naturally, both of lords and others of court, that I took it ill," but Beeston placated Herbert and promised that the poet would trim away all the offensive matter.[22] Obviously the public theaters and their playwrights were still feeling the wrath of their courtly enemies, and by the end of the year a new barrage was fired from a different quarter: the manuscript of William Prynne's *Histriomastix,* the most powerful of Puritan attacks on the stage, was in circulation.

Chapter Six

The Massinger Caroline Plays, 1632–1639

Having made a full defense of the moral function of drama in *The Roman Actor* and joined with his colleagues in a full attack on those who would turn the art of the public theater to privileged superficiality, Massinger responded to the new threat of Prynne's *Histriomastix* in 1632 with a rich, entertaining comedy that defies any accusation of immorality or superficiality. Perhaps, however, the new attack that came from a citizen rather than a courtier influenced Massinger to write a play closer to *A New Way to Pay Old Debts* than to any of his other plays and to dramatize, in the realistic setting of city life, the threats to the basic morality of citizen and gentleman alike. The threats posed by the veneration of the superficial splendor and sensual pleasures of life and the unscrupulous, expedient means of acquiring them were being fought simultaneously on three different battlegrounds of English life by three very different groups: the professional dramatists in their battle with the "plush and velvet poets," many of the parliamentarians in their battle with the Crown, and the Puritans in their battle with the Church of England.

The City Madam

In *The City Madam* Massinger employs the signifying names of the comedy of humors, the social satire of the comedies of city life, and contrapuntal variations of similar themes played out on various social levels. The citizen class is represented, in the main, by the central set of characters, the family of the wealthy merchant Sir John Frugal: his pretentious, social-climbing wife, their two spoiled daughters, and his brother Luke, living on Sir John's charity after having been imprisoned for debt after wasting his patrimony. The aristocracy is represented by Lord Lacie and his son, Sir Maurice, who seeks the hand and dowry of one of the Frugal daughters. The

country gentry is represented by Master Plenty who seeks the hand
and dowry of the other Frugal daughter. The apprentices, young
Goldwire and Tradewell, the steward Holdfast, and various others
represent the service class. And the underclass of pimps, bawds,
prostitutes, and thieves is dramatized in the scenes with the wench
Shavem and her colleagues and customers. Cheating, expedient hypocrisy for quick gain, is the motive for the actions of each of these
social classes within the play.

Massinger skillfully interweaves two interdependent plots. The
central characters involved in both the plot of the wooing of the
Frugal daughters and in the plot of the proving of Luke are present
in the first scene. Lady Frugal and her two daughters, preparing for
the first visit of young Lord Lacie and Master Plenty, alternate
between their pretentious concern for fashions more elegant and
manners more ostentatiously delicate than those of any court lady
and their reviling of the daughters' Uncle Luke, who is treated as
a recalcitrant drudge expected to earn every shred of their grudging,
patronizing charity.

The sympathy for Luke, evoked by his patient acceptance of such
rude treatment at the hands of his brother's family, increases when,
stepping in between his brother and three who are unsuccessfully
begging him to extend their loans, Luke makes an impassioned and
persuasive plea for placing mercy above mere money and for seeking
goodwill rather than hard interest. The senior Lord Lacie, after
witnessing this scene, is moved to advise Sir John that he is doing
himself a disservice in allowing Luke to be treated as anything other
than a noble brother who has fallen on hard times. Sir John is
skeptical, but seems to agree.

The sympathy thus evoked and reinforced is then put into question
and Luke's hypocrisy begins to be revealed when he praises Lady
Frugal's profligate expenditure of her husband's hard-earned money
for an extravagant display at table, belittles the prudent husbandry
of the steward Holdfast, instructs his brother's apprentices, young
Goldwire and Tradewell, in methods of dipping into their master's
till, and seductively describes to them the pleasures of dressing like
a gallant, catching all eyes in an ordinary, and having one's way
with wenches, all of which can be had at once with just a little
money stolen here and there from their rich master.

The false values, immorality, disregard for basic human relationships, and shoddy expediency of Luke's instruction are variously

dramatized in the succeeding scene of courtship. Both the young Lord Lacy and Master Plenty are courting dowries and have not even determined which daughter is to marry which suitor, although Sir John, also more interested in connections than kinship, is ready to sign papers of jointure and portions before such determination is made. Lady Frugal insists that a prognostication of the marriages be made by her astrologer, Stargaze, who, not unpredictably, predicts in the mystifying language of charts and trines that the acquisitive daughters will have absolute sovereignty in their marriages.

Anne will wed Lord Lacy only if he promises to provide her a coach and six, footmen, gentlemen ushers, a private box at the theater, and other absolute necessities. Mary informs Master Plenty that although she prefers country pleasures to the city pleasures required by her sister, those pleasures do not include supervising a dairy house or barnyard fowl and acting as a drudge to an ale-drinking overlord who spends his leisure riding to the hounds; all the rents, manors, stock, even the children are to be exclusively hers.

The same values that inform the courtship scene inform the first brothel scene. Shavem and her bawd Secret lament the lack of trade in the oldest profession. Shavem, like the Frugal daughters, longs to drive around like an elegant lady in a fine coach, and this requires many more customers than just Goldwire who comes to her whenever he can steal the price of admission from his master. A band of outlaws force their way in and would take from Secret what she sells to others, but are thwarted by Goldwire who comes in disguised as a justice of the peace, accompanied by a constable who is in fact Dingem the pimp.

In a further parody of the Frugal daughters and their suitors, Shavem, using the blackmail of specific crimes, forces the thieves to admit her sovereignty and to kiss the soles of her shoes before she allows them to escape. Dingem then credits the "prentice gallant" with the best head for tricks and seeks to enhance Shavem's value by recounting all her offers of marriage. Goldwire's query, "offers of marriage?" provides an occasion to reinforce the parodic parallels of the play:

> *Dingem.*   Yes Sir, for marriage and the other thing too.
> The commoditie is the same. An Irish Lord offer'd her
> Five pound a week.

Secret.   And a cashier'd Captain, half
          Of his entertainment.

Dingem.   And a new made Courtier
          The next suit he could beg.

                                              (3.1. 80–84)

Goldwire is won to pay his stolen money for Shavem's new gown,
a petticoat, appurtenances, servants, banquet, and caudle.

The plot for the testing of Luke is worked out secretly between
Sir John and Lord Lacie as a means of bringing Lady Frugal and the
daughters to their senses, of bringing the disgusted suitors back to
their courtship, and of justifying or disproving Sir John's negative
judgment of his brother. The plot begins with Lord Lacie's coming
to the Frugal household with word that Sir John has retired to a
monastery and has entrusted his brother Luke with the management
of his household and all his fortune.

Luke uses the same pattern of response to all who then sue to
him, beginning with Lady Frugal who begs him not to be vengeful
in his treatment of her or her daughters, despite their earlier treatment of him. Luke cheerfully promises even more than is asked,
gives nothing, and then takes away all that was already possessed.
Luke promises Lady Frugal and her daughters that they shall have
even more extravagant attire and insists that they put aside their
rude dress that he may make them the rivals of Roman matrons.
He then provides them with only the simplest clothes, dismisses
all the servants, and prohibits all vanity.

Luke promises the messengers that come from Tradewell, who
has run up gambling debts, and Goldwire, who owes Shavem money,
that he will bring all the money they need to Shavem's the next
day. He arrives the next day with sheriffs and marshals, has the
apprentices, gamesters, and bawds arrested, and seizes all the property that has been paid for out of "his" funds. Luke listens to the
schemes, plans, and expectations that will allow Hoyst, Penurie,
and Fortune to pay their debts if they are given a further extension
of their loans. He then cheerfully bids them meet him at the Exchange the next day, at which time he forecloses on them all, has
them thrown into prison, and seizes on their schemes and turns
them to his own profit.

There is only one request that he does not seem to agree to with
immediate, hypocritical cheerfulness, and that is Sir John's request

that he house and convert the three Indians (actually Sir John, young Lord Lacie, and Master Plenty) brought to the house by Lord Lacie. Luke swears that he cannot afford to feed them, that Sir John's fortune had been greatly overrated. Luke complies, however, when Lord Lacie warns him that if Sir John's wishes in this matter are not carried out that good gentleman might return. Luke, who before his brother's departure had constantly mouthed pieties and spent all his leisure in prayer, now openly reveals that he worships no god but mammon, and is overjoyed when he learns that the Indians in their native land worship a similar god, one that will provide him with a second fortune if he makes the proper sacrifice. Luke hesitates only for a moment and then agrees that sending his sister-in-law and nieces to Virginia to be human sacrifices to the Indian mammon is little enough to exchange for a second fortune.

In the final scene Luke reveals himself as the very personification of all-consuming avarice, the spoiled daughters become loving maidens, the city madam becomes repentant and forgiving, and Lord Lacie becomes wiser. After demanding a thousand pounds each from the apprentices' fathers and warning Lord Lacie that he holds a mortgage on his estate, Luke attends his elaborate birthday dinner, one he particularly enjoys because he has not paid for it. He is mildly amused at the entertainment prepared for him, unmoved at the pageant of all those he has made miserable by his grinding avarice, and insists it is no feat for his entertainers to present images of Sir John, young Lacie, and Master Plenty before which the sadder but wiser ladies make their tender repentant farewells—unless those images could take life. Of course they do. Lord Lacy admits Sir John had been right in his appraisal of Luke; the young couples pledge marriages of devotion rather than display; Sir John offers to submit Luke to full punishment, but Lady Frugal begs clemency for him, for he has taught her a vital lesson.

Reputation, Records, and the Mystery of the Prologue

The success of *The City Madam* in its own day has been thrown into question by the prologue of *The Guardian*, licensed for performance in October 1633. The prologue suggests that Massinger, after two stage failures, had not brought a play to the stage for the past two years. These suggestions seem to be in direct contradiction to the evidence of Massinger's theatrical activity for 1631 and 1632: four new plays licensed, a play presented at court, and *The City Madam* licensed only the year before.[1] How then is one to read the prologue? What is one to make of Massinger's career in the light of these words:

> After twice putting forth to Sea, his Fame
> Shipwrack'd in either, and his once known Name
> In two years silence buried, perhaps lost
> I'th the general opinion; at our cost
> (A zealous sacrifice to Neptune made
> For good success in his uncertain trade)
> Our Author weighs up anchors, and once more
> Forsaking the security of the shore,
> Resolves to prove his fortune: What 'twill be,
> Is not in him, or us to prophesie;
> You only can assure us. Yet he pray'd
> This little in his absence might be said,
> Designing me his Orator. He submits
> To the grave censure of those abler Wits
> His weakness; nor dares he profess that when
> The Critiques laugh, he'l laugh at them agen.
> (Strange self-love in a writer!) He would know
> His errors as you find 'em, and bestow
> His future studies to reform from this
> What in another might be judg'd amiss.
> And yet despair not, Gentlemen; though he fear
> His strengths to please, we hope that you shall hear
> Some things so writ, as you may truly say
> He hath not quite forgot to make a Play,
> As 'tis with malice rumour'd. His intents
> Are fair; and though he wants the complements
> Of wide-mouth'd Promisers, who still engage
> (Before their Works are brought upon the Stage)
> Their parasites to proclaim 'em: This last birth
> Deliver'd without noise, may yield such mirth,
> As ballanc'd equally, will cry down the boast
> Of arrogance, and regain his credit lost.

No one has presented a satisfactory explanation for the dilemmas created by this poem.

If the prologue is taken as a literal statement of fact, how is one to explain the evidence of the theater records? If the "two years silence" is accurate, then what is to be made of the four plays licensed and the four plays published in 1631 and 1632?[2] If there were two failures immediately preceding a two years' silence, then they must have been before the closing of the theaters in April 1630, and would suggest that Massinger's plays were not succeeding at precisely the moment that Carew and his coterie were suggesting that undiscriminating audiences preferred Massinger's plays to those of Davenant. Edwards, in his introduction to *The Guardian*, points out that there is no squaring the prologue with the evidence, and Edwards and Gibson in their general introduction to Massinger's works reject the possibility that the prologue is attached to the wrong play as a rather "desperate solution" because Massinger seems to have had no two-year period of silence once his career was launched.

Suppose, however, that the prologue were attached to the wrong play by the wrong author, that it had, in fact, been written for a play by someone other than Massinger. Humphrey Moseley owned the printing rights to *The Guardian* and brought it to print for the first time in 1655, fifteen years after Massinger's death. Since Moseley had acquired the printing rights to many plays in addition to those by Massinger, it is possible that he, accidentally or deliberately, placed someone else's prologue with Massinger's play. Among the many Moseley titles of plays of this period, plays not printed before the closing of the theaters, there is one play by a playwright who in fact had two failures and a two-year period of silence before that play was performed. The possibility that the prologue printed with *The Guardian* was written for that play provides an interesting and logical solution to the problem.

The prologue to *The Guardian* seems particularly appropriate for *News from Plymouth* by William Davenant and to the course of Davenant's career in the theater.[3] Davenant had been silent for two years before 1633 because he had been out of the city, seriously ill and under the care of the queen's physician. Davenant had had two stage failures before his enforced retirement from the stage, and one of those failed plays had been printed with a wholesale attack on the popular theater. Given the coordinated, united reaction of the professional theater to Davenant's attack, it seems unlikely that any play of his could have succeeded on the stage of the Globe or Blackfriars, no matter how much courtly support he mustered, without some public admission by Davenant that he had bitten the hand he hoped would feed him. *News from Plymouth* is a nautical

comedy that would make the initial nautical metaphor of the prologue appropriate, and the prologue in its entirety bears a marked
resemblance to a large slice of humble pie, or crow, fashioned for
public consumption. That Davenant made his peace with the King's
Men and the popular audience is evident; that he would not have
printed his own public act of contrition along with his other works
after the theaters reopened and he himself was in control of the
King's Men seems equally evident.

In any event, no matter how desperate this solution may sound,
it is possible that Davenant's prologue for *News from Plymouth*, a
Moseley property, was printed as the prologue to Massinger's *The
Guardian*, another Moseley property, and that possibility provides
a more logical reading of the recorded course of the careers of both
Massinger and Davenant. By the time Davenant returned from the
country, Massinger and his fellow playwrights had rallied the support of the acting companies, their theater audiences and reading
public, their own powerful advocates at court and beyond, and were
successfully united against the greater attack posed by Prynne's
Histriomastix.

The king was quick and vicious in his reaction to Prynne, and
the Inns of Court joined together to demonstrate their full support
of theater by preparing and performing the extravagant masque, *The
Triumph of Peace*, written by James Shirley, main playwright for
Queen Henrietta's Men and colleague, ally, and friend of Massinger.
By October 1633, when *The Guardian* was licensed for performance,
the great masque was all the talk of London, and it was performed
at court in February 1634, less than a month after a court performance of *The Guardian*.

On 12 January 1634, according to the Master of the Revels, "*The
Guardian*, a play of Mr. Messengers, was acted at court . . . by
the Kings players, and well likte."[4] And, although it has been
suggested earlier that *The Emperor of the East* had a court performance,
Herbert's entry about *The Guardian* is the first extant record of an
official court performance for one of Massinger's independent plays.
Several of his unidentified collaborations with Fletcher had been
performed at court over the years, and *The Fatal Dowry*, written
with Field, had been performed there on 3 February 1631. It is not
known, however, whether Massinger's part in that play was identified at the time of its court performance or not; the only designation
of authorship on the title page of 1632 is "Written by P. M. and

N. F." The title page of that play advertises neither Massinger's name nor the fact that the play had had a court performance. It is not illogical, therefore, given the only available evidence, to assume that the court presentation of *The Guardian* marked Massinger's first official court recognition, his formal court debut.

A court performance of a play by Massinger, who had written all but two of the new plays licensed for the King's Men since the attack on the professional theater began in 1629, followed a month later by a great masque by Shirley, who was the mainstay of Queen Henrietta's Men, would certainly seem a triumphal vindication of the tastes, values, and achievements of the professional dramatists and the theater companies that brought their plays to life. It is hard to believe that by the end of the next year the opposing faction had gained control over the King's Men and dominated their selection of plays until the closing of the theaters. After 1634 Massinger never again wrote more than a play a year for the King's Men.

In 1634, however, the fifty-one-year-old Massinger began a triumphal year with his day in court. The play chosen, or selected, bows to court tastes in its inclusion of two masquelike interludes: the wedding entertainment prepared as a welcome for Caliste, and the forest entertainment presented as a welcome for Iolante. However, the play, called a "Comical-History" on its 1655 title page, proves to be a solid example of the drama defended by Massinger and his fellow playwrights despite its pastoral masques and plots of love and honor.

The Guardian

The Guardian is a merry, simple play with serious, complex undertones. Although the name of the play refers to the jovial, lusty, hunting, swearing, wenching Durazzo, guardian to his chaste young nephew, Caldoro, who is single-minded in his service to love rather than lust, the play centers in the main on the family of Severino.

Severino, long banished for having killed his brother-in-law in a duel and now living in Robin Hood fashion as king of a band of outlaws in the forest outside Naples, has left his wife Iolante and their daughter Caliste to live as widow and orphan in Naples. Iolante, inordinately proud of her own chastity, rigorously controls the life of Caliste who has fallen in love with the unprincipled young gallant, Adorio, and rejects the honorable attentions of Caldoro.

Most of the play involves the contrasting course and accidental assurance of the chastity of Iolante and Caliste. Caliste has declared her love for Adorio, who has told her in no uncertain terms that he might love her but will not marry her, and she has firmly rejected Caldoro despite his having roundly beaten Adorio for his insulting rejection and proposition. After her mother restricts her to quarters and forbids her even to look out the window at a gentleman, Caliste takes the advice of her maid Mirtilla and sends her to Adorio with a jewel and a letter entrusting her chastity to his care and begging him to help her run away from her mother's home. Adorio is transformed by Caliste's letter and vows to steal her away and marry her. Mirtilla is transformed at the sight of Adorio and becomes the rival of her mistress.

Adorio and his attendants come to rescue Caliste at about the same time that Caldoro, Durazzo, and their attendants come to abduct Caliste; Caldoro's guardian can take his nephew's melancholy no longer. In the confusion of darkness and fantastically plotted romances, Caliste goes off with Caldoro thinking he is Adorio, and Adorio takes Mirtilla off to wedding festivities and discovers just before vows are to be exchanged that he has the maid, not the maiden. The two parties, weary and camped close to each other, are all beset with a magical weariness. Caldoro chastely guards Caliste while she sleeps; Adorio falls asleep with his head in Mirtilla's lap; Durazzo wakes, brings Caliste and Caldoro to witness Adorio and Mirtilla sleeping together, and Caliste's former love for Adorio immediately becomes love for Caldoro. All are then captured by outlaws.

Meanwhile, Iolante, encouraged by her flattering and lascivious confidant, Calypso, succumbs to the attractions of a visiting nobleman, and, not recognizing that he is, in fact, her own brother, not dead, but in service to the General of Milan under the name Monteclaro, invites him for a midnight rendezvous. Under the guidance of Calypso, Iolante prepares an elaborate and seductive welcome for her mysterious lover on the same night that her daughter runs away, on the same night that her husband slips into Naples in disguise to visit his wife. Severino arrives first, meets Monteclaro at the door, delays him by pretending to be the watch, and then confronts Iolante. Not believing her story that she always prepares a banquet, perfumes the chamber, and wears a filmy nightdress on their anniversary, Severino binds his wife and then waits in another chamber until he can take her with her lover. Calypso comes to announce Monteclaro, finds Iolante bound, and agrees to swap places with her while Iolante sends Monteclaro away. Calypso as Iolante's substitute encounters the full wrath of Severino who bursts into the dark chamber, stabs her in the arm, and bites off her nose.

While Severino is searching for his wife's lover, Iolante returns, much chastened by the sober words of her dismissed caller, releases Calypso, resumes her position as the bound wife, and prays loudly and vehemently that her arm be healed and her nose restored since she has been injured for a crime that she has not committed. Severino's skepticism as he hears her prayers before he enters her chamber becomes passionate penitence when he finds his wife untouched by any mark of his rage. Iolante is noble and immediate in her forgiveness. After a quick and futile search for their daughter and Mirtilla, Severino and Iolante gather up all her jewels and slip away to his forest kingdom.

All is resolved and explained in the final gathering of all the persons of the play in the forest court of Severino. Caliste and Caldoro are allowed to wed. Adorio, learning that Mirtilla is the orphan of an old companion of Severino and, therefore, of gentle birth, takes her for his wife. Monteclaro reveals that he had repeatedly and irrationally provoked Severino and deserved to have been defeated by him; and, obviously, Severino is not guilty of his murder. The king learns that the outlaws have robbed no honest man nor touched any woman, but have only taken from those who exploit and prey on others. Love and honor are restored.

While most of the action alternates between the daughter's quest for a husband and the mother's battle with temptation, the title of the play directs attention to the contrast of Durazzo's licensed and careless government of his ward and Severino's regulated and disciplined control of his outlaw kingdom. The fictional kingdom of Naples is one in which chaste matrons are more faithful in words than deeds, one in which the wanton gallant is preferred over the devoted servant, and one in which a guardian can advise his ward that a "fresh and lusty" pleasure comes at the end of each full day of hunting and hawking:

> I'll give thee a Ticket,
> In which my name, *Durazzo's* name's subscrib'd,
> My Tenants Nutbrown daughters, wholsom Girls,

At midnight shall contend to do thee service.
I have bred them to't; should their Fathers murmure,
Their Leases are void; for that is a main point
In my indentures.
(1.1. 343–47)

The model kingdom of the play is the exiled kingdom of Severino,
one under his absolute rule but governed by a Table of Articles that
insures protection and justice for all. It is in Severino's kingdom
that the predominant false values of Naples (pointedly similar to
the predominant false values of England) are rejected and that the
problems of Naples and of the play are resolved.

In addition to the didactic and topical considerations suggested
by the title and the structural contrasts, the play provokes some
interesting and puzzling questions. Is there some analogical function
for Iolante's incestuous desire for her brother? The situation is left
peculiarly unexplained in the play. At the end when it is revealed
that Monteclaro is her brother, Iolante says,

Now, Sir, I dare confess all:
This was the ghest invited to the Banquet,
That drew on your suspition.
(5.6 219–21)

This explanation might satisfy her husband, but not an audience
who has heard her losing battle with her own adulterous desire for
Monteclaro. And is it coincidence that Massinger has a character
lose a nose in a play that appeared just months after Davenant
reappeared in London without a nose? Or did Massinger, like so
many poets and playwrights for the rest of Davenant's life, use that
loss to gain a wicked laugh from an audience that quickly made an
association with Davenant's plight?

The year, 1634, particularly the initial month, must have seemed
as bleak for Davenant as it was glorious for Massinger. Davenant,
who had returned to London in the final months of 1633 with his
face deformed by his illness and his property sequestrated for a
murder conviction, submitted his first new play to the Master of
the Revels and had it severely censored only days before the court
performance of *The Guardian*. Davenant, however, still had powerful
friends at court, and Herbert records that the king himself, at the
insistence of Endymion Porter, reviewed the censored matter and

allowed much of it, but instructed Porter and Davenant to go through the motions of resubmitting the play to Herbert and receiving it, civilly, from his hands.[5] Even the king's intervention, however, could not save that play from derision at Blackfriars, derision Davenant details in more than one poem;[6] the play, however, was performed at court less than a month after *The Guardian.* The year may have begun bleakly for Davenant, but the twenty-eight-year-old son of an Oxford innkeeper, with no long theatrical apprenticeship behind him, with no history of theatrical success, using the methods Massinger had attacked from the stage for twenty years, made his debut at court in the same month as Massinger.

The year, 1634, however, held other triumphs for Massinger. The now-lost *Tragedy of Cleander* was licensed the first week in May and performed before the queen at Blackfriars the following week. This play is generally considered to be either a revision of *The Lovers' Progress* or *The Lovers' Progress* itself as it stands in the Beaumont and Fletcher folio; the prologue to that play indicates that it had been so thoroughly revised that it required a license as a new play. And, as mentioned earlier, *The Lovers' Progress* has many of the platonic trappings of a Caroline play.

In June 1634 the King's Men performed Massinger's *A Very Woman,* described in its prologue as a revision of some earlier, unidentified play. Scholars are in general agreement that *A Very Woman* is Massinger's revision of a lost play by Fletcher, a play in which Massinger may have had an earlier hand. However, Massinger does not mention Fletcher in the prologue as he generally does when his old master had a hand in a play, and no existing play by Fletcher bears any resemblance to *A Very Woman.* The prologue declares that Massinger revised the play at the request of his patron, but since the play was first published fifteen years after Massinger's death and includes no dedication, the identity of that patron remains unknown.

The 1633 quarto of *A New Way to Pay Old Debts,* the last of Massinger's plays to be printed before the initial performance of *A Very Woman,* was dedicated to the earl of Carnavon, son-in-law to Philip Herbert, earl of Pembroke and Montgomery, to whom Massinger had dedicated *The Bondman* in 1624 and to whom he addressed a poem of condolence, "Sero, Sed Serio," on the occasion of the death of Herbert's son in 1636. Massinger's father had spent his life in service to the Herbert family—Massinger mentions that association in his dedications to *The Bondman* and to *A New Way to*

Pay Old Debts—and Aubrey claims that Herbert gave Massinger a small pension that was paid to his wife after Massinger died. Whether the "Patron" who requested *A Very Woman* was some member of the Herbert family or the King's Men themselves—for whom Massinger had written so much and who must have owned the old play that Massinger revised—remains a mystery. In any event, the "new play" that Massinger brought to the Blackfriars stage in June 1634 is a play that one can only hope had a happier reception in its own day than it has had with many subsequent critics, particularly those of our day.[7]

A Very Woman

The central situation of the play, a noble woman rejects a noble lover and plights her troth with a slave (the slave turns out to be the noble lover she had previously rejected), is treated in various ways in various plays by Massinger and by other playwrights in the same period. Massinger's treatment of that situation in *A Very Woman* deserves particular attention in relation to his other treatments, to the treatments by other playwrights, and to subsequent critical reaction.

The "very woman" of the title is Almira, the imperious, beautiful daughter of the viceroy of Sicily. None of her many noble suitors can rival the eligibility of Don John Antonio, the prince of Tarent, nor can any rival the magnificence of his royal courtship. Almira, however, rudely rejects his attentions and chooses instead Don Martino Cardenes, son of the duke of Messina. When Almira's brother, Pedro, a close friend of Don John and in love with Leonora, kinswoman to Don Martino, brings his sister a jewel from Don John and entreats her to give his noble friend a farewell audience, Almira refuses the request and tosses the jewel to Don Martino's page.[8]

Pedro accuses his sister of uncivil ingratitude and urges Don John to see her despite her refusal. When Don John arrives he finds that Almira has departed, but Don Martino, irrationally jealous even though he has won Almira and will wed her on the next day, is waiting to taunt his defeated rival with every insult possible. Bearing it all coolly and nobly until Don Martino strikes him, the prince then draws his sword and floors Don Martino. Almira rushes in, flies into a wild, grieving rage, grabs up a sword and wounds Don John. Don Martino's father, the duke, passionately insists on immediate revenge, torture, death. Almira's father, the viceroy, imposes the voice of reason, refuses to touch the prince without a fair trial, and when Don Martino shows some sign of life, chides the duke for demanding revenge before he attends to the life of his son. At Pedro's almost forcible insistence, Don John escapes Sicily by ship, and Paulo, a physician whose powers are considered supernatural despite insistence that he abjures all charms other than his art and prayer, comes to attend Don Martino whose wound is not as threatening as his melancholy (that approaches madness). Almira, too, is near madness and assures the revenge-starved duke that she will live only until she can see the prince sacrificed on the tomb of Don Martino. When word of Don John's escape reaches the court, the duke accuses Pedro and the viceroy of complicity, forbids Leonora to see Pedro again, and puts Leonora under the guard of the comically dipsomaniacal Borachia, wife of the foolish Cuculo.

Borachia's insistence that she must have "a well-timbered slave" to help her guard her charge and Paulo's need for actors in the drama of Don Martino's recovery send Cuculo and the doctor to the slave mart where Don John and the captain of their captured ship are up for sale as slaves. Cuculo buys Don John to assist his wife in guarding Leonora and Almira, who is confined with Leonora since that young woman is the only one who seems able to help Almira maintain even a vestige of her sanity.

Neither Almira nor Pedro recognize Don John, but both recognize the noble qualities of the slave who soon discovers that a sufficient quantity of fine Greek wine for Borachia makes it possible for Pedro to gain access to Leonora and for Almira to learn the history of the slave she finds so strangely attractive. In hearing his story, she reviews her own past treatment of Don John with chagrin. Almira's progress from derangement to a reasonable appraisal of her past behavior and a rejection of the values that determined that behavior is paralleled by Paulo's slow but effective treatment of Don Martino. Using a series of moral psychodramas, Paulo is able to guide Don Martino from his life-threatening guilt for his scurrilous provocation of a noble prince to peaceful health disturbed only by his desire to beg forgiveness of the prince.

All comes to a tragicomic climax and resolution when the pirates, who had captured Don John and the captain and sold them into slavery, attempt an abduction of two rich prizes, the daughters of the viceroy and the duke, Almira and Leonora. Don John, the noble slave, saves them and is rewarded with civic garlands in the presence of the entire company, but is sent off to prison under sentence of immediate death when Almira insists that she must marry him. Don John, in prison, resumes his princely attire, provided by the captain who, together with one of Paulo's slaves, reveals to all the story of his capture and enslavement. Don Martino begs the prince's forgiveness and relinquishes his claim to Almira. Almira is abashed that she had rejected the prince she came to love as a slave, but joyful that he does not reject her now. Leonora and Pedro are united. Paulo sends Cuculo and Borachia, who are banished from the court, a cure for drunkenness.

Both the similarity of the central situations of *A Very Woman* and *The Bondman* and the difference in the treatment of those situations are immediately apparent. In *The Bondman* Cleora remains strictly faithful to a secretly dishonorable lover until his unjustified jealousy and admission of his earlier commitment free her to entertain love for the noble slave. In *A Very Woman* Almira, after rejecting Don John when he paid suit as a noble prince, loves him as a slave, and is fortunately released from her pledge to Don Martino after she has already decided that she will marry Don John. To focus on Almira's "lightness," as some critics do, in contrast to Cleora's constancy, or to assume that the play is a poor patch of old scenes of merry license from Fletcher and an unsuccessfully imposed moral structure by Massinger is to miss many interesting features and suggestions of this play.

First, there are extended similarities and differences between *The Bondman* and *A Very Woman*, written ten years apart, and both dedicated to the Herbert family. In both plays the brother of the heroine seeks to determine the marriage of his sister. In *The Bondman* Cleora's brother gives full support to Leosthenes, the lesser suitor, and prevents Pisander, who has come in royal suit, from ever having an audience with Cleora. In *A Very Woman* Almira's brother supports the prince in opposition to Don Martino and arranges an audience, albeit an unsuccessful one.

In *The Bondman* the real slaves are enslaved by their own servility; they, like their corrupt masters, are cruel creatures of appetite, and only incited to noble action in their own behalf by the passionate rhetoric or forceful demand of their moral superiors; they have the mentality of slaves and cringe back to servitude at the threat of the whip. The slaves in *A Very Woman* are all enslaved by force and sold for profit, four of them play nonservile roles in the later action of the play, and the catalogue of persons for sale in this "comic" scene includes a sampling of representative English types as well as the intriguing pair of nine-year-old black twins who are sold to sing as blackbirds in a cage. The hero of *A Very Woman*, unlike the hero of *The Bondman*, actually *is* a slave despite his royal birth and noble nature.

Massinger's very different treatment of very similar material and the use of similar materials and thematic treatment by William Cartwright in *The Royal Slave*, 1636, and by Aston Cokayne in *The Obstinate Lady*, 1642?, suggests, perhaps, that toward the end of the first decade of the reign of Charles I it was not merely appetite or attitudes of servility that enslaved men, but the rule of those who were themselves the slaves of passions, irrational codes, and stubborn blindness. The only truly free man in *A Very Woman* is the thief who is too mean and self-serving to be bought or sold; it is he who provides the plan for kidnapping the two noble maidens, protected by only a fool, a drunk, and a slave. If the beautiful, much-sought bride of this play, like so many others, suggests England herself, then *A Very Woman* dramatizes a nation already diseased and in need of a healing physician.

Perhaps it is the sense of a deeply diseased nation, a nation sick from poor care and governed by equally diseased caretakers, that motivates the parallel portraits of the distraction and restoration of Almira and Don Martino. Massinger dramatizes not just the disease, but the cure, and that cure is no magical, quick-fix elixir. The play dramatizes the slow step-by-step stages that the characters must go through before health is restored. They must experience dramatic encounters with their own past actions and consider alternative courses of future behavior before they can see clearly and act rationally. Massinger, perhaps, never dramatized the full, rich psychological complexity of an individual character, but he repeatedly dramatized the curative process that restores the mental or spiritual health of a character.

Massinger's models of dramatic psychotherapy may have been meant for both the nation and its individual citizens. The doctor in *A Very Woman* is Paulo, the sister of protected virtue in *The Renegado* is Paulina, Camiola's confessor in *The Maid of Honour* is Paulo; all share a consistently wise and guiding voice like that of Paulina in Shakespeare's *Winter's Tale*. Variations on the name Paul allowed the playwrights to echo the pulpit and underscore the paths to virtue that are the same in the Acts of the Apostles and in the acts of many of the plays that strutted their brief hour upon the stage. Whether these thoughts haunted Massinger's mind or not can never be known. Certainly in the years to follow he had good reason to believe that the King's Men, the company he had served and that had served him for twenty years, had become a royal slave forced to make the surface of drama ever more gorgeous and the substance ever more ephemeral. In 1635 Massinger had a single drama licensed for the King's Men. His now-lost *The Orator* was licensed in January. Davenant had two plays licensed and a masque performed at court. Blackfriars performed plays imported from court, including Killigrew's *The Conspiracy*, performed with scenery imported from the court production. Meanwhile, some unspecified "company of roguish players" performed Massinger's *A New Way to Pay Old Debts* in the provinces.

Massinger's last extant play was licensed for the King's Men on 9 May 1636, but since the theaters were closed three days later because of plague and did not reopen until October 1637, it probably did not come to the stage until after that date. *The Great Duke of Florence* was entered in the Stationers' Register for publication in 1635 and printed in 1636 with a dedication to Sir Robert Wiseman that includes the lines,

But it is above my strength, and faculties, to celebrate to the desert, your noble inclination, (and that made actuall) to raise up, or to speak more properly, to rebuild the ruines of demolish'd Poesie. But that is a worke reserved, and will be, no doubt, undertaken, and finished, by one that can to the life expresse it.

Beyond the conventions of dedications, Massinger seems to be addressing a need beyond his own individual art, a despair about the state of poetry in general.

The Bashful Lover

Despair and the dark undertones of tragic vision that reverberate in the complex parallels of *The Bashful Lover* make this tragicomedy one of the bleakest plays in Massinger's canon. The "happy resolution" comes only after war has ravaged the kingdom and scourged the countryside, ambition and greed have dishonored the innocent, jealousy has exiled noble service, and lust has destroyed friendship. Beauty and chastity are a bright beacon that beckons destruction. The ending is a fairy-tale resolution; the only Court of Love that could resolve the forces unleashed in *The Bashful Lover* exists only in the dream wishes of man's imagination.

The beautiful Matilda, daughter of Gonzaga, duke of Mantua, is sought by all and demanded on penalty of war by Lorenzo, duke of Tuscany. All the others who seek Matilda for themselves band together to serve her, to defeat Lorenzo, and to bolster their own claims. Uberti, prince of Parma, chief in rank among her suitors, is fiercely supported in his claim, as in all things, by his true friend, Farneze, kinsman to Gonzaga. Galeazzo, the bashful lover (actually the heir to Milan but in Mantua simply as an unidentified gentleman) the most diffident and reverently devoted of Matilda's suitors, vows to bring the defeated Lorenzo in bonds to the feet of Matilda.

Uberti's outrage that a mere gentleman would dare to offer his service to Matilda or to share in the exploits of those of exalted rank and Matilda's gracious acceptance of and high praise for any who offers noble service suggests that Massinger is again employing the noble-slave triangle that he used in *The Bondman* and in *A Very Woman*. In addition, a further comparison with *The Bondman* and other of Massinger's earlier plays is invited by the Ascanio-Alonzo subplot.

Ascanio (the name of the legendary heir destined to reclaim Troy/England, frequently used by Massinger and Fletcher during the Jacobean years) is the assumed name of Matilda's adored young page. Ascanio is actually Maria, the young daughter of Octavio, the most deservedly honored general of Milan until Gonzaga, jealous of the success of Octavio, banished him from the realm. During Octavio's palmy days in Milan, Alonzo, kinsman of Lorenzo, considering an alliance with Octavio's family as a quick and easy means to wealth and power, seduced Maria and promised to marry her but then abandoned her when her father was banished. The noble maid abandoned for a more promising alliance is a trope Massinger uses again and again and one that generally suggests the rejection of virtue in the service of appetite or ambition.

With the onset of hostilities, Ascanio, having recognized Alonzo as the messenger from Lorenzo, deserts Matilda and becomes the page of Galeazzo, who is the wonder of the war. Galeazzo repays

Uberti's insult by saving his life; saves the life of Gonzaga, who desperately misses the service of Octavio and regrets his unwarranted banishment; and has Alonzo at the point of death when Ascanio begs that his life and honor be spared and that he be allowed to go free. Since Ascanio has begged this boon for the enemy in the name of Matilda, Galeazzo frees Alonzo, who vows vengeance for the dishonor.

All Galeazzo's valor, however, cannot stem the tide of Lorenzo's forces. With defeat at hand, Galeazzo goes into self-imposed exile as love's martyr, Matilda is sent to a distant fort, Gonzaga and the others put off their royal robes and adopt the garb of shepherds, and Lorenzo gives the order to fire the woods, scourge the countryside, and capture Gonzaga that he may be subjected to torture. Galeazzo, forced to seek succor for the faint and starving Ascanio who has refused to leave his side, stumbles into the rude dwelling of Octavio, and there witnesses the reconciliation of father and daughter.

The friendship of Alonzo and Pisano, in service to Lorenzo, is dramatized as a contrast to the friendship of Uberti and Farneze, in service to Gonzaga. Farneze, isolated behind enemy lines but protected by the coat of a dead Florentine, finds Uberti, unprotected, gives his friend the Florentine coat, and goes forth to face death. Alonzo and Pisano capture Farneze, fall into an argument about which one deserves the ransom until Lorenzo comes in and orders them to make peace and to execute Farneze immediately. Before they can comply with Lorenzo's orders, Uberti, assumed to be a Florentine because of his coat, dashes in, pretends to recognize Farneze as the one who slaughtered Uberti's family, sees Farneze's sword in a soldier's hand, and begs to be allowed to kill Farneze with his own slaughtering sword. The ruse works, and Farneze and Uberti escape.

Alonzo and Pisano, hoping to avoid Lorenzo's wrath over the escape of Farneze, set out from their camp and spy the bright beauty of Matilda that shines like a comet on the hillside as she tries to reach the fort. They have no sooner captured her, however, than they fall to quarreling about which of them is entitled to ravish her. Matilda begs them to fight the lust that is threatening both her and them, but they prefer to bind her to a tree and fight each other. Galeazzo, armed with nothing but a shepherd's crook, discovers them, seizes Pisano's sword when Alonzo fells his friend, turns on Alonzo, reminds him that they have met before, and strikes him down. Matilda recognizes her bashful lover, but Galeazzo does not recognize her until she reveals her identity in response to his assurance that she owes her life to the power of Princess Matilda who owns all his service and provides all his power. When Galeazzo finds he is facing Matilda, he begs her forgiveness for having failed to bring all her enemies to the dust. Matilda forgives him and offers a kiss as his reward. He will only kiss her foot.

Octavio and Maria find the wounded Pisano and Alonzo and tend their wounds. In a variation of Massinger's familiar scene of healing, Octavio takes the guise of a friar, solicits a confession from Alonzo of his dishonorable treatment of Maria, repentance for that treatment, and a willing agreement to restore her lost honor by marrying her.

Meanwhile, one of Lorenzo's men captures Matilda and Galeazzo and takes them to Lorenzo who, at the first sight of Matilda, is so smitten that he becomes her penitent servant, declares a general peace, promises restitution for the damage done to her realm, and gives her absolute power in all things. Gonzaga, in gratitude, offers Matilda to Lorenzo, but neither Uberti nor Galeazzo will submit to this condition. It is agreed that all will be settled in a Court of Love. Matilda, of course, chooses Galeazzo, and even as Farneze is complaining that the heir of Mantua should marry no one less than a duke, a messenger from Milan arrives and announces that Galeazzo's brother is dead and Galeazzo is now absolute lord of Milan. All are peacefully reunited and Matilda urges Lorenzo to pit his mighty powers against the Turks and to make no more wars among Christians.

For one who comes to this play with Massinger's canon freshly in mind, there is the appalling realization that at the end of the play the uxorious Galeazzo is the duke of Milan! The wheel comes full circle. *The Bashful Lover*, for all that it is called tragicomedy, includes less mirth than many tragedies. There is none of the old-boy wit of Durazzo or the hypocritical lascivious chat of Calypso of *The Guardian*, or the slapstick comedy of the drunken Borachia in *A Very Woman*. Gothrio, the lean and greedy servant of Octavio, perhaps elicited a few laughs in performance but seems to function more as a low, parodic variation on the theme of avaricious appetite.

The signals of the play in general are confusing. The dominant import of the play is unalleviated destruction and loss despite all good intentions and noble service. Lorenzo's sudden capitulation to Matilda's beauty, unbelievable enough after three acts of his military tyranny, is made even more unbelievable by coming so shortly after her capture and threatened rape by Alonzo and Pisano. The opposition of true and noble service and the false veneration of rank, established so clearly in the beginning and in the actions of the play, is then undercut at the end by the discovery that Galeazzo is noble in title as well as service. But this isn't much; one suspects that the ubiquitous discovery that the desirable lowborn are really highborn is a convention that allowed playwrights to have their democratic cake and continue to eat, too.

Perhaps Matilda represents a land, an England, so glorious that all should serve her, and all outside forces indeed seek to claim her, even if she is raped in the attempt. And in Maria/Ascanio is a parallel portrait of that same land, fathered by its best defenders, fathered by one now banished and living in anguish because his daughter has been dishonored and cast aside by one who wanted only her wealth and power and who abandoned any loving service, duty, or care. Perhaps the reconciliation of the ideal and the actual could be considered only as a dream, a distant dream eternally deferred. The dark image of destruction overshadows even a stage representation of the dream. The Jacobean whistle in the dark of the court performance of *Pericles* back in 1619 had grown very faint by 1637.

All that remains of Massinger's work after *The Bashful Lover* is a scrap of a play, a few titles, and his dedication to *The Unnatural Combat*. Herbert's notes about Massinger's only recorded title for 1638 suggest that Massinger continued to serve those who preferred a warning whistle of alarm to a mollifying whistle in the dark:

Received of Mr. Lowens for my paines about Messenger's play called *The King and the Subject*, 2 June 1638, . . . The name of *The King and the Subject* is altered, and I allowed the play to bee acted, the reformations most strictly observed, and not otherwise, the 5th of June, 1638.

At Greenwich the 4 of June, Mr. W. Murray, gave mee power from the king to allowe of the play, and tould me that hee would warrant it.

> "Monys? Wee'le rayse supplies what way we please,
> "And force you to subscribe to the blanks, in which
> "We'le mulct you as wee shall thinke fitt. The Caesars
> "In Rome were wise, acknowledginge no lawes

"But what their swords did ratifye, the wives
"And daughters of the senators bowinge to
"Their wills, as deities," &c.

This is a peece taken out of Phillip Messengers play, called *The King and the Subject,* and entered here for ever to bee remembered by my son and those that cast their eyes on it, in honour of Kinge Charles, my master, who readinge over the play at Newmarket, set his marke upon the place with his owne hande, and in thes words:

"This is too insolent, and to bee changed.'

Note, that the poett makes it the speech of a king, Don Pedro, king of Spayne, and spoken to his subjects.[9]

Some scholars have suggested that the title was changed to *The Tyrant,* a title included in Moseley's list of 1653, but Bentley agrees with Greg's observation that if Herbert considered *The King and the Subject* a censurable title, he would not have preferred *The Tyrant.*

The king censored Massinger and made Davenant laureate. Ben Jonson had died in 1637, John Ford wrote his last play in 1638, and Massinger, the only remaining playwright whose writing roots went back to the early Jacobean years, continued to produce a play a year for the King's Men, but those plays are lost. Only the titles remain in Herbert's records: 25 September 1639, *Alexius, or The Chaste Lover {Gallant};* 26 January 1640, *The Fair Anchoress of Pausilippo {or The Prisoner?}.* In 1639, the year after Davenant became laureate and the year before Massinger died, Massinger brought his old tragedy, *The Unnatural Combat,* to press.

In both his choice of this play and in his dedication Massinger seems to look back to the beginning of the decade, back to the battle of the play books, prologues, and manuscript responses of the early 1630s, a battle that Massinger had been able to win only as long as Davenant was off the scene. The sensational subject matter of *The Unnatural Combat* is probably closer in kind to the early plays of Davenant than any of Massinger's early plays, and Massinger, perhaps, chose to remind his reading public that such melodramatic tragedies of lust and blood as those he had written years before had taken Davenant far on the road to high acclaim. After three failed plays in this kind and two years off the scene, Davenant returned

and, within six years, had replaced Massinger as primary playwright
for the King's Men, taken Jonson's place both as author of court
masques and as laureate, and acquired the management of the players
at the Phoenix.

Why hadn't Massinger's great achievement in the same kind taken
him further? His dedication for *The Unnatural Combat*, perhaps,
explains; in some instances it is not what one writes, but who does
the underwriting. In the opening lines of his dedication to Anthony
St. Leger, Massinger writes, "That the Patronage of trifles, in this
kinde, hath long since rendered Dedications, and Inscriptions ob-
solete, and out of fashion, I perfectly understand, and cannot but
ingenuously confesse, that I walking in the same path, may be truly
argued by you of weaknesse, or wilfill errour."

The inclusion of the word "ingenuously" signals the relation of
this dedication to the battle carried on in dedications and commendatory verses in the beginning of the decade, for "ingenuous,"
used and conflated with "ingenious," is a term that haunts all the
exchanges of that battle. [10] Heeding the signal and looking at this
final dedication in relation to "the Patronage of trifles, in this kind,"
one is led back to the relation of patrons to Davenant's early "trifles
in this kind."

Davenant's first three trifles were dedicated to the earl of Somerset
(the infamous Robert Carr, forever banished from court, along with
his wife, for their complicity in the murder of his friend, Thomas
Overbury), Lord Weston (who had lost his position as High Treas-
urer of England and had died in disgrace since Davenant's dedication), and the earl of Dorset (the queen's Lord Chamberlain, one of
the "roaring boys" of the previous reign who served as a model for
many of Davenant's strongest supporters, and according to a later
description by the earl of Clarendon, "the vices he had were of the
age, which he was not stubborn enough to contemn or resist"). [11]
Such a display of patrons of high power and low values addressed
in the opening pages of embarrassing juvenilia that had in fact
received their real patronage from a court coterie that shared and
exploited the absolute rule of that court could well make both
patrons and poets beyond that coterie reluctant to have their relationship expressed in print.

Later in the dedication Massinger further recalls the quarrel that
began with inflated acclaim for plays that were poor copies of works
like *The Unnatural Combat:*

I present you with this old Tragedie, without Prologue, or Epilogue, it being composed in a time (and that too, peradventure, as knowing as this) when such by ornaments, were not advanced above the fabricque of the whole work.

This passage proved mysterious and confounding until the recovery of the 1630 prologue to *The Maid of Honour,* a prologue that seems to have drawn more attention and response than the play, a prologue that isolated Massinger as a specific target in a battle that seems to have begun as a generalized broadside against the controlling tastes of the public theater.

The dedication to *The Unnatural Combat,* the last surviving document of Massinger's career in the theater, was written a year before his death and three years before the death of London theater as he had known it, helped shape it, and fought for it. The theater of the Restoration belonged to Davenant.

Chapter 7
Conclusion

To exhume a playwright buried under more than three hundred years of the sands of time and to set him in living motion in the theater of his day is a consummation divinely to be wished and eternally to be denied. Assured denial should not thwart the attempt, particularly when the playwright is Massinger, who has been subjected to repeated metaphorical burials. Martin Butler's account of the publication of the works of Beaumont and Fletcher as an act of Royalist propaganda in 1646 illustrates a metaphorical interment of at least a decade of Massinger's works. [1]

The burial metaphor was drawn from an odd epitaph written by Massinger's friend, Sir Aston Cokayne, who seems to have made the only objection to that persuasive attribution of all of Massinger's collaborative work with Fletcher and all Fletcher's independent work to those newly made Siamese twins "Beaumont and Fletcher." Wood's account of Massinger's burial, given earlier, has Massinger buried in the churchyard close to the playhouse attended by the comedians. Cokayne provides a different and more intriguing locations for Massinger's burial:

An Epitaph on Mr. John Fletcher, *and Mr.* Philip Massinger, *who lie buried both in one Grave in St.* Mary Overie's Church *in* Southwark.

> In the same Grave *Fletcher* was buried here
> Lies the Stage-Poet *Philip Massinger:*
> Playes they did write together, were great friends,
> And now one Grave includes them at their ends:
> So whom on earth nothing did part, beneath
> Here (in their Fames) they lie, in spight of death. [2]

These lines, generally accepted as literal, may be metaphorical.

Cokayne may have meant to suggest that the achievement and fame of Fletcher and Massinger were in fact indistinguishable. With the death of Massinger, who had continued in the tradition that

118

they had shared, the actual achievement of their shared art was buried while the fabulous achievement of a single creature, "Beaumont 'n Fletcher," created by the compilers and appreciators of the Beaumont and Fletcher Folio, emerged to replace a now-dead tradition. The tradition of Fletcher and Massinger was buried in the same grave. There is a metaphorical accuracy to the lines even if they are literally correct.

The conclusion that a tradition of drama, shared by Massinger and Fletcher and perpetuated by Massinger, could be buried along with Massinger would seem to contradict the earlier insistence that the audience, not the author, determines the nature of the plays that succeed or fail on the stage. There is no contradiction. Censorship of plays, the imposition of court-sponsored plays, and the importation of court plays distort the selection available to the audience and ultimately change the nature of that audience. The audience of the mid-Jacobean years was an audience that read and relished complex, multilevel patterns of signification; they understood that language as automatically as they understood the street cant and "roaring" that no one can understand today.

Of course there were the natural, albeit irrational, shifts in taste and pleasure, and the desire for old wine in new bottles, particularly since a repertoire theater insured the continued availability of old wine in old bottles. Massinger learned the craft of playmaking in the years when Shakespeare was still writing new plays for the Globe and Blackfriars and, on occasion, collaborating with Fletcher. In that time and from those masters Massinger learned to fashion the stuff of the stage to the tastes and desires of the age. Those tastes and desires became offensive to a new order of rule that used its power to obliterate them.

All drama is political in some sense of the word, and the drama of Massinger is political in several senses of the word. First, Massinger's plays, like all plays, automatically reflect the values of his time. Second, his plays perpetuate a received tradition of multilevel drama that addresses issues of morality as they pertain to the soul of man, the fate of the realm, and the divine order. In addition, it seems probable that Massinger discovered, early on, that he could command an audience with outspoken dramatic attacks on specific political issues or events and that, subsequently, his audiences came with the expectation that he would make such attacks and, perhaps, learned to read them even when they were not outspoken.

The assumption that Massinger's drama was political and might
be dangerously so was shared in his lifetime. When Herbert censored
Davenant's *The Wits,* he crossed out oaths (which the king allowed
as "asservations"); when he stopped the performance of a revival of
Fletcher's *The Tamer Tamed, or The Woman's Prize,* it was for "foule
and offensive matters," i. e., "oaths, prophaness, and publique
ribaldry"; when he censored Massinger's *Believe as You List* and *The
King and the Subject,* it was for political reasons. Massinger's reputation for treating touchy matters may have been established early
with his part in *Sir John van Olden Barnavelt* and *The Second Maiden's
Tragedy* and the lost *Spanish Viceroy,* if it were indeed Massinger's.

Something in Massinger's plays beyond identifiable politically
offensive matter disturbed those in the court of Charles I. Political
matter could be forbidden; a multilevel manner that allowed the
artificial fictions of popular drama to be read politically required
other means of obliteration. The court support of Davenant proved
to be one method of silencing Massinger and changing, not just the
taste of the audience, but the audience itself. Most of Davenant's
plays were licensed directly to him, and presumably the fee was
paid by his patrons at court; Massinger's plays were licensed to the
playing company that judged them to have sufficient drawing power
to be worth the required fee. Those who came to cheer Davenant
and hiss Massinger attracted their own imitators who quickly adopted
the taste of the court faction and, consequently, never learned to
understand or delight in the complex, multilevel manner of Massinger's plays.

Cokayne was right. Massinger was buried in the same grave with
Fletcher. The Fletcher that was resurrected and venerated by the
Royalists in 1646 is not the Fletcher whose plays delighted the
Jacobean stage. All the playwrights of those Jacobean years—Shakespeare, Jonson, Dekker, Middleton, Marston, Webster, Ford, and
Massinger—shared such a precise understanding of the conventions,
structures, and functions of their art that they easily joined with
each other in various combinations to create collaborative plays that
are seamless fabrics. When Massinger died, there was no living voice
trained in that tradition, and the words of Fletcher and of Massinger
and Fletcher were turned to the service of many of the false values
they had fought against in those words. The Royalists lost the war,
but won the theater. Massinger's plays became the property of those

he had opposed. Massinger and his art have come down to us through the hands of his enemies.

In order to recover either Massinger or his art, one must strive to read with the eyes of his times. His plays and the other plays of his age, read in relation to each other and to other written discourse of the age, can provide a vocabulary of many of the methods and patterns of signification shared by the authors and audiences of Massinger's day. The more one knows of an age the easier it is to share and understand the art of that age. The fears and dreams, the heroes and villains, the gossip and great issues, the commonplaces and the common causes of the greater stage are the crucial context of any play in any age.

Reading Massinger in his literary and historical context provides entertainment and the pleasure of intellectual exercise. Tracing the dramatic protests against the ills of his age in Massinger's popular plays may also provide understanding of the role of popular drama in our own age. The conflicts Massinger dramatizes, the values his plays vindicate, and the evils that threaten those values are our own.

In addressing Sir Anthony St. Leger in the dedication to *The Unnatural Combat*, Massinger speaks of his patron's father:

Your noble Father, Sir Warham Sentliger (whose remarkeable vertues must be ever remembered) being, while hee lived, a master, for his pleasure, in Poetry, feared not to hold converse with divers, whose necessitous fortunes made it their profession, among which, by the clemency of his judgment, I was not in the last place admitted.

Massinger defines those "remarkeable vertues" and describes them in active opposition to the vices of the age in the elegy written, one assumes, shortly after the death of Sir Warham in October 1631. This elegy was printed for the first time in 1978 by J. H. P. Pafford who discovered the poem in a manuscript commonplace book that belonged to John Clavell, who wrote a commendatory poem for Massinger's *The Emperor of the East*.[3]

In his praise of Sir Warham St. Leger, as in all the plays of his long career, Massinger poses the struggle of the seven deadly sins and the seven cardinal virtues, not as a contest of black and white abstractions on a morality chessboard, but as those abstract sins and virtues inform the specific choices and actions of a specific life in a specific moment of history. The noble life, Massinger insists in elegy and drama, depends not on birth but on merit, and merit is the active realization of faith, hope, love, prudence, fortitude, justice, and temperance and the successful resistance to pride, envy, wrath, sloth, avarice, gluttony, and lust.

In his elegiac description of St. Leger, as in so many of his plays, Massinger bodies forth the combined virtues of hope, prudence, fortitude, and justice in the image of a soldier who successfully resists all that would keep him at his fireside when duty calls. St. Leger, according to Massinger, did not make getting and spending the main aim of his life. He did not purchase commands or preferments. His large deserts earned him the noblest favors, and he shared these and his own unencumbered, inherited income with those who were in need. Massinger celebrates his charity and his rejection of avarice and greed.

Massinger describes St. Leger's refusal to seek court preferment in terms familiar from his plays: "he ever held obsequyousnesse the disease / and rust of active virtue." Words, according to Massinger's elegy, served the brightness of active virtue. St. Leger defended his faith with his words as actively as he had defended his country with his sword. He engaged in learned arguments with divines and used all his powers to force atheists to confess to a higher power. St. Leger also found his prudent pleasure in the words of his conversation, his storytelling, and his poetry writing.

In elegizing St. Leger, Massinger has also elegized his own life and art, an art that actively defends virtue and attacks the evils that threaten virtue. Massinger was a man of the word who used words for all the pleasures of stage conversation and storytelling, for arguments and persuasion, and for the defense of faith.

Notes and References

The historical information for this study has been gathered from a wide variety of sources, and sources are not cited except for quotations or detailed incidents. The fullest, easily accessible history of the Jacobean years is G. P. V. Akrigg, *Jacobean Pageant or The Court of King James I* (New York: Atheneum, 1967); there is not an equivalent account of the Caroline years. The following are some of the texts used for information and background: Thomas Birch, *Court and Times of Charles I* (London: H. Colburn, 1848) and *The Court and Times of James I* (London: Coburn, 1849); Quentin Bone, *Henrietta Maria: Queen of the Cavaliers* (Urbana: University of Illinois Press, 1972); John Bowle, *Charles I: A Biography* (London: Weidenfeld and Nicolson, 1975); *The Letters of John Chamberlain,* ed. N. E. McClure (Philadelphia: American Philosophical Society, 1939); C. H. Firth, *The Memoirs of Edmund Ludlow* (Oxford, 1874); Antonia Fraser, *King James VI of Scotland, I of England* (New York: Knopf, 1974); S. R. Gardiner, *History of England from the Accession of James I to the Outbreak of the Civil War 1603–1642* (London, 1883–84) and *The Personal Government of Charles I . . . 1628–1637* (London: Longman's, Green & Co., 1877); Elizabeth Hamilton, *Henrietta Maria* (London: Hamish Hamilton, 1976); Roger Lockyer, *Buckingham: The Life and Political Career of George Villiers . . . 1592–1628* (New York: Longman, 1981); B. Manning, ed. *Politics, Religion, and the English Civil War* (London: Edward Arnold, 1973); Richard L. Ollard, *The Image of the King: Charles I and Charles II* (New York: Atheneum, 1979); [F. Osborne], *Historical Memories on the Reigns of Queen Elizabeth and King James* (London, 1658); V. Rowe, "The Influence of the Earls of Pembroke on Parliamentary Election," *English Historical Review* 50 (1935):253–56; Lawrence Stone, *The Causes of the English Revolution, 1592–1642* (New York: Harper & Row, 1972) and *The Crisis of the Aristocracy* (Oxford: Oxford University Press, 1967); Agnes Strickland, *Lives of the Queens of England,* vol. 5 (London: Longman, Brown, Green, Longman, & Roberts, 1857); R. M. Smuts, "Henrietta Maria in the 1630s," *English Historical Review* 93 (1978):26–45; I. A. Taylor, *The Life of Henrietta*

Maria (London: Hutchinson, 1905); C. V. Wedgewood, *Poetry and Politics Under the Stuarts* (Cambridge: Cambridge University Press, 1960); Charles Williams, *James I* (New York: Roy, 1953); George C. Williamson, *Lady Anne Clifford, Countess of Dorset, Pembroke & Montgomery, 1590–1676* (Kendal: Titus Wilson & Sons, 1922); David Harris Wilson, *King James VI and I* (New York: Holt, 1956); *The Secret History of K. James I and K. Charles I* (London, 1690).

Preface

1. Philip Edwards and Colin Gibson, "General Introduction," in their edition of *The Plays and Poems of Philip Massinger* (Oxford: Clarendon Press, 1976), xlv; all references to the plays, title pages, dedications, commendatory verse, and Massinger's poems are cited from this text, hereafter referred to as PPM.

2. Gerald Eades Bentley, *The Jacobean and Caroline Stage* (Oxford: Clarendon Press, 1941–68); hereafter cited as Bentley, *Stage.*

3. Philip J. Finkelpearl, "The Role of the Court in the Development of Jacobean Drama," *A Quarterly for Literature and the Arts* 24 (1982):138–58.

4. Martin Butler, *Royal Slaves? The Stuart Court and the Theatre, Renaissance Drama Newsletter: Supplement* 2 (1984), and *Theatre in Crisis, 1632–1642* (Cambridge: Cambridge University Press, 1983).

Chapter One

1. The main sources for the biographical information are Edwards and Gibson, "General Introduction" and Commentary in *PPM;* Donald Lawless, *Philip Massinger and his Associates* (Muncie, Ind.: Ball State University, 1967); and T. A. Dunn, *Philip Massinger* (Edinburgh: Thomas Nelson, 1957). Additional information about both the Massingers and the Cromptons (Massinger's mother's family) has been drawn from *Transactions of the Bristol and Gloucestershire Archaeological Society* 13 (1890):376–77; 14 (1891):332; 16 (1893):143,161; 21 (1898):138–42; 23 (1900):125–26; 24 (1901):316–19; 28 (1905):333; 56 (1934):156, 201–26; 61 (1939):281–82, hereafter cited as *TBGAS; Alumni Oxonienses . . . 1500–1714*, ed. John Foster, vol. 1; *Alumni Cantabrigienses*, John Venn and J. A. Venn, comps., part 1; *Calendar of State Papers, Domestic, 1581–1590; Calendar of Records for the Corporation of Gloucester*, W. H. Stevenson, comp., 1893, 44, 64–70; W. P. W. Phillimore and Leland L. Duncan, eds., *A Calendar of Wills Proved in the Consistory Court of the Bishop of Gloucester, 1541–1650*, 1895, 98, 121, 223.

2. Donald S. Lawless, "Arthur Massinger of London," *Notes and*

Queries 7 (1960):29–30; Donald S. Lawless, "The Parents of Philip Massinger," *N&Q* 15 (1968):256–58; Mark Eccles, "Arthur Massinger," *TLS*, 16 July 1931, 564; James Phelan, "Philip Massinger," *Anglia* 2 (1879):1–64. The Countess of Pembroke, wife to Sir Henry Herbert and mother to Sir William, was the sister of Sir Philip Sidney, for whom, it has been assumed, Philip Massinger was named.

3. Phelan, "Philip Massinger," see n. 2; Dunn, *Massinger*, 4–6.

4. Donald S. Lawless, "Anthony Crompton (c. 1561–?), Uncle of Philip Massinger," *N&Q* 29 (1982):408–9; Donald S. Lawless, "Anne Massinger and Thomas Crompton," *N&Q* 4 (1957):416–17; A. L. Browne, "Title Deeds in the Manor of Prestbury, Gloucestershire," *TBGAS* 61 (1939):281–82; *C. S. P., Domestic, 1581–1590*, 696. Pembroke in a dispute with Essex over property in Gloucester relegated the matter to Arthur Massinger (see nn. 2,3); Crompton was one of Essex's representatives in this same matter.

5. Anthony à Wood, *Athenae Oxonienes* (1691) 1:536; Gerard Langbaine, *Account of the English Dramatick Poets* (1691), 352–53.

6. In his commendatory poem to Massinger's *The Emperor of the East*, Singleton addresses Massinger as "true friend and kinsman." In addition to those biographical sources cited in note 1, there are references to Singleton in the following: John Aubrey, *Aubrey's Brief Lives*, ed. by Oliver Lawson Dick (Ann Arbor: University of Michigan Press, 1962), 280; John MacLean and W. C. Hearne, *The Visitation of Gloucestershire* (1885), 100–1; Stevenson, *Calendar of Records . . . Gloucester*, 69; *TBGAS* 24 (1901):293–307; 30 (1907):91–121; John Washbourn, *Bibleotheca Gloucestrensis* (1824), cvi, 77, 152.

7. The letter that serves as the source of this information is reprinted in full in *PPM*, vol. 1: xvii; since the letter is actually three short notes signed separately by Nathan Field, Philip Massinger, and Robert Daborne, it is generally referred to as the "tripartite letter."

8. Aston Cokayne, "A Chain of Golden Poems," in *Small Poems of divers sorts* (London: printed by Wil. Godbid, 1658. The relevant portions are cited in *PPM*, vol. 1: xix–xx; Lawless, *Associates*, 17; Bentley, *Stage*, 4:753. Lawless, *Associates*, 18, also cites Langbaine as further confirmation of Massinger's collaboration with Fletcher.

9. Accounts of the Dramatic Companies rely on Bentley, *Stage*, 1: passim. Bentley's monumental work informs almost every page of this study and serves as the source for facts concerning licensing and publication of plays, court performances, actors, other playwrights, plague closings, and other records relating to the theater of the period; in addition, his interpretation of these facts is frequently accepted and incorporated.

10. Bentley, *Stage*, 2:590–92.

11. *PPM* 1: xxxii–xxxiii, 9. The Harbord volume, now in the Folger

Library, contains all Massinger's plays printed before 1633 except *The Virgin Martyr*, corrected in his own hand, evidently in preparation for a printed collection that was never made or as a presentation volume to a patron. Edwards and Gibson provide the fascinating account of the history of the volume.

12. Reprinted in *PPM*, 1:xvii.

13. Reprinted in part and in full in *PPM*, 1:xviii; 4:389–91.

14. *PPM*, 1:xxiii–iv, provides the full list of Moseley's titles, discussion of the problem, and further bibliography. In subsequent pages Edwards and Gibson discuss the problem of John Warburton's list that may be no more than a copy of Moseley's entries in the Stationers' Register. The problem, not herein addressed, is also addressed by Bentley, *Stage*, 4:749–830, in relation to titles of plays attributed to Massinger.

15. Cyrus Hoy, "The Shares of Fletcher and His Collaborators in the Beaumont and Fletcher Canon," *Studies in Bibliography*, (1956–62); Bertha Hensman, *The Shares of Fletcher, Field and Massinger in Twelve Plays of the Beaumont and Fletcher Canon* (Salzburg, 1974). Despite Hoy's claim that linguistic habits provide an unquestionable basis for determining Massinger's share of the Beaumont and Fletcher plays, Hoy, like so many others before him, relies on internal evidence of style, and such evidence is unreliable. Too little is known about habits and methods of collaboration in the seventeenth century, about copying practices and variations (did the author always write down his own lines? did an author ever dictate to a collaborator? to a scribe?), and about the various stages in the life of a script that belonged to and was performed by an acting company with varying membership and for different audiences over a long period of time. The arguments made by Samuel Schoenbaum in *Internal Evidence and Elizabethan Authorship* (Evanston, Ill.: Northwestern University Press, 1966) still hold. Therefore, in addition to including those plays attributed in part to Massinger by Hoy, this study also includes those attributed by others: E. K. Chambers, *Elizabethan Stage* (Oxford: Clarendon Press, 1933), 3:215–35; Bentley, *Stage*, 3:305–433; and A. H. Cruickshank, *Philip Massinger* (Oxford: Oxford University Press, 1920), 151–62. Hoy, Hensman, and Edwards and Gibson provide more conservative lists. *Bonduca*, not included by any of those cited above, is included here because an existing manuscript of the play is done in a hand that is also present in the manuscript of *Believe as You List* and *An Honest Man's Fortune*. Two plays included in many of the lists, *Henry VIII* and *Two Noble Kinsman*, have been omitted because they are so fully discussed in relation to the works of Shakespeare.

16. See Bentley's discussion of *The Laws of Candy*, in *Stage*, 3:355–56, for some of the problems of attribution and an acid opinion of the methods of attributers or "distintegrators."

17. John Aubrey, *The Natural History of Wiltshire*, ed. J. Britton, (1847), 91; cited in *PPM*, 1: xxxv.

18. Peter Beal, "Massinger at Bay: Unpublished Verses in a War of the Theatres," *Yearbook of English Studies* 10 (1980):190–203.

19. *Athenae Oxonienses*, ed. Philip Bliss, (1813–20), 3:776; cited in Bentley, *Stage*, 4:757.

Chapter Two

1. Unless one has their chronology very firmly in mind, Beaumont and Fletcher, from the following passage, would seem to have been frequent guests in the court of Charles I: "But he [Charles I] enjoyed the playwrights most of all and particularly, perhaps, Beaumont and Fletcher. He had seen *The Knight of the Burning Pestle* as a young man; it exactly matched his sense of humour and the two dramatists were much in demand at his Court. He possessed a collected edition of their plays and, as he loved to do, made a list of the titles with his own hand." This is from a recent, recommended biography, *King Charles I* by Pauline Gregg (London: J M Dent, 1981), 190. Gregg must have meant that their *plays* were much in demand, but the passage is misleading. In addition, Charles could not have cherished the collected works for very long since it was first printed in 1647, after Charles was already in captivity and only two years before his execution.

2. Butler, *Theater and Crisis, 1632–1642,* 9–11.

3. In addition to information about and discussions of the attribution of these plays by Chambers, Bentley, and Hoy, as cited in n. 15, chap. 1, see the introductions to the following editions: John Fletcher, *Bonduca*, ed. W. W. Greg (*The Malone Society Reprints*, 1951); *The Second Maiden's Tragedy*, ed. Anne Lancashire (Baltimore: John Hopkins University Press, 1978); *The Honest Man's Fortune*, ed. J. Gerritsen (Groningen: J. B. Walters, 1952); the other plays are available in collections of the plays of Beaumont and Fletcher.

4. "Speech to Parliament," 1604, *The Printed Political Works of James I*, ed. Charles McIlwain (Cambridge: Harvard University Press, 1918), 272; also cited by Anne Lancashire in the introduction to her edition of *The Second Maiden's Tragedy* (Baltimore: Johns Hopkins University Press, 1978) in which she describes and advocates very similar principles of allegorical reading. Butler (*Theatre and Crisis,* 6), considering a slightly later period, also advocates a similar method; after citing censorship of a play in 1620 that had no correspondence with a particular situation or obvious allegorical significance Butler goes on to say, "It was often in devices of this kind, that work not through direct statement or allegory but through analogy and oblique reflection—mirrors for magistrates, in fact—that dramatists reflected the political concerns of 1632–1642."

128 PHILIP MASSINGER

5. Vivian Ridler, ed., *The Faithful Friends* (Oxford: Oxford University Press for the Malone Society, 1975).

6. Akrigg, *Jacobean Pageant*, 177–204; *A Complete Collection of State Trials and Proceedings for High Treason and Other Misdemeanours* (London: 1776), 1:328–58; *The Secret History of K. James I and K. Charles I . . .* (London, 1690), 21–23. Lois Potter, in a Special Session on Tragicomedy at the 1983 convention of the Modern Language Association, concluded that the Somerset scandal served as one of the most profoundly disturbing events in the national life long after the Civil War and that the scandal was often recalled in the drama of the Interregnum. See also Vernon F. Snow, "Essex and the Aristocratic Opposition to the Early Stuarts," *Journal of Modern History* 32 (1960):224–33; Anne Lancashire, *"The Witch:* Stage Flop or Political Mistake?" in *"Accompaninge the Players": Essays Celebrating Thomas Middleton,* ed. Kenneth Friedenreich (New York: AMS Press, 1983), 161–81. Lancashire also includes a discussion of the dramatic conventions of allegorical drama and the masque.

7. The associations with Raleigh were strengthened by the general knowledge of the late Prince Henry's reliance on Raleigh as a mentor.

8. Edwards and Gibson *(PPM)* discuss the sources of *The Fatal Dowry* in the introduction to that play, 1:1–12. They provide source studies and the bibliography for additional source studies in the introductions to all of the plays in the Massinger canon.

9. Wilhelmina P. Frijlinck, ed., *Sir John van Olden Barnavelt* (Amsterdam: H. G. Van Dorssen, 1922), discusses the censorship and the ambiguity of the changes in the introduction to the play.

Chapter Three

1. Akrigg, *Jacobean Pageant*, 271.

2. Edwards and Gibson *(PPM)* review the source studies for Massinger's canon in introductions to the individual plays; Bentley, *Stage,* includes sources for the collaborations with Fletcher in the section on Fletcher, 3:305–433. Eugene M. Waith treats Seneca as a source in both *"Controversia* in English Drama: Medwall and Massinger," *PMLA* 68 (1953):286–303 and *The Pattern of Tragicomedy in Beaumont and Fletcher* (New Haven: Yale University Press, 1952).

3. For a complete list of the plays that include a character named Ascanio see T. L. Berger and W. C. Bradford, Jr., *An Index of Characters in English Printed Drama to the Restoration* (Englewood, Colo.: Microcard Editions Books, 1975).

4. G. P. Gooch, *Annals of Politics and Culture* (Cambridge: Cambridge University Press, 1901), 114.

5. Prologue to an adaptation of Shakespeare's *The Tempest* by John Dryden and William Davenant; cited in Bentley, *Stage,* 3:414.

Chapter Four

1. The fact that *The Fatal Dowry*, a property of the King's Men, was not printed until more than a decade after it was written is generally considered an indication of its value as a stage property; the play was also selected for court performance in 1631. *The Virgin Martyr*, although it went into two editions in Massinger's lifetime, was attractive enough for a revival with revisions in 1624.

2. *PPM*, 1:105–6; Eva A. W. Bryne, "Introduction," in her edition of *The Maid of Honour*, xxxiii–xxxv.

3. This opinion is shared by Bentley, *Stage*, 4:798.

4. Samuel Rawson Gardiner, "The Political Element in Massinger," *The New Shakespere Society's Transactions, First Series*, no. 4 (1875–76), 316–19.

5. *PPM*, 1:201–3.

6. Thomas Whitfield Baldwin, "Critical Introduction" in *An Edition of Philip Massinger's "The Duke of Milan,"* 21–22. *Othello* was Shakespeare's second most popular play of this period, according to *The Shakespeare Allusion-Book*, ed. E. K. Chambers (London: Oxford University Press, 1932).

7. Inga-Stina Ewbank, "Realism in Jacobean Tragedy," a lecture at the Folger Shakespeare Library, 8 February 1982.

8. *PPM*, 1:303; Benjamin Townley Spencer, "Introduction" in his edition of *The Bondman*, 28–43.

9. Spencer, "Appendix 1," *The Bondman*, 257–59; Butler, *Royal Slaves? The Stuart Court and the Theatre*, Renaissance Drama Newsletter: Supplement Two (1984).

Chapter Five

1. See Bentley, *Stage*, 3:336–39, 387–91, for discussion of these two plays. Although Massinger may well have had a hand in *The Fair Maid of the Inn*, his independent plays of these years must lay claim to all available space.

2. *PPM*, 4:397–405.

3. Knowledge of the quarrel is not new, and partial accounts are available; without complete records of the age, all accounts must remain partial accounts. See Bentley, *Stage*, 1:26,224–25; 3:204–5, 449–50; 4:816–17; 5:1115–18; Michel Grivelet, " 'Th'Untun'd Kennell': Note sur Thomas Heywood et le Théâtre sous Charles Ier," *Etudes Anglaises* 7 (1954):101–6; George Bas, "James Shirley et 'Th'Untun'd Kennell': une petite guerre des théâtres vers 1630," *Etudes Anglaises* 16 (1963):11–22; Peter Beal, "Massinger at Bay: Unpublished Verses in a War of the Theatres," *Yearbook of English Studies* 10 (1980):190–203; *PPM*, 4:414–15.

4. For a full account of Davenant see Bentley, *Stage*, 3:193–225; Philip Bordinant and Sophia B. Blaydes, *Sir William Davenant* (Boston: Twayne Publishers, 1981); Arthur H. Nethercot, *Sir William D'avenant, Poet Laureate and Playwright-Manager* (Chicago: University of Chicago Press, 1938).

5. *Albovine*, for which there is no record of performance, was printed without license in 1629; *The Cruel Brother*, licensed for performance in 1627, and *The Just Italian*, licensed for performance in October 1629, were both entered in the Stationers' Register on 10 January 1629/30, or 1630 by our calendar.

6. *The Dramatic Works of Sir William D'Avenant*, ed. James Maidment and W. H. Logan (London: Sotheran & Co., 1872), 1:207; all Davenant allusions are from this edition.

7. Pauline Gregg, *King Charles I* (London: J M Dent & Sons, 1981), 421, 426, 428; it is pure speculation to assume that Davenant wrote the verse himself, but it is a speculation based on a similar conclusion by Peter Beal about the authorship of the anonymous response to Massinger's prologue to *The Maid of Honour*.

8. Thomas Carew, "To my worthy Friend, M. D'avenant, upon his excellent Play, *The Just Italian,*" in *Works of D'Avenant*, 1:205–6; reprinted by Bentley, *Stage*, 1:224–25.

9. Bentley, *Stage*, 1:26; see n. 3 for other accounts of the quarrel.

10. Cited by Beal; see n. 3 for full reference.

11. Bentley, *Stage*, discusses the rarity of cast lists at several places; the discussion is initiated with his consideration of *The Roman Actor*, 4:816–17.

12. Thomas Carew wrote a poem, "To Ben. Iohnson. Upon occasion of his Ode of defiance annext to his Play of the new Inne," after Jonson published the play with the ode in 1631; the poem informs Jonson that he is past his zenith and moving into a decline. *The Poems of Thomas Carew*, ed. Rhodes Dunlap (Oxford: Clarendon Press, 1949), 147.

13. Russ McDonald, "High Seriousness in Popular Form" in *Philip Massinger: A Critical Reassessment*, ed. Douglas Howard (Cambridge: Cambridge University Press, 1985), 83–116.

14. Bryne, in the Introduction to her edition of the play (London: for Bryn Mawr, 1927), xxiii–xxxii, provides a retrospective of these contradictory designations, and Edwards in his Introduction to the play (*PPM* 1:105), points out that on the basis of topical allusions Gardiner assigned the play to 1631 and Bryne to 1623. John Monck Mason, notes and commentary in his edition of *The Dramatick Works of Philip Massinger* (London, 1779).

15. See, particularly, Bryne, Introduction, ix–xxii.

16. Rhodes Dunlap, in the introduction to his edition of Carew's

poems, describes Carew's successful efforts to win Elizabeth Sheldon for Kit Villers, Buckingham's younger brother; also see William Habington's poem "To a Wanton," with its allusion to Carew's "The Rapture," *English Seventeenth-Century Verse,* ed. Richard S. Sylvester (New York: W. W. Norton, 1964), 2:427.

17. *Aubrey's Brief Lives,* ed. Dick, 86.

18. Thomas Birch, *The Court and Times of Charles I* (London: Henry Colburn, 1848), 1:439–40.

19. Dunlap, in his introduction to *Poems of Thomas Carew,* repeats a story of Carew's having walked in on the queen and Sir Henry Jermyn in an embrace, and simply disappeared as though he had seen nothing; Jermyn's gratitude for his silence is considered one source of Carew's power at court. Obviously, however, Carew did not remain completely silent, or the account would not be available today. Henrietta Maria's biographer, I. A. Taylor, *The Life of Henrietta Maria* (London: Hutchinson & Co., 1905), 1:110, admits that there was gossip about the queen and Jermyn, but nothing was ever proven. Massinger may have intended to suggest that the queen was innocent and that Carew maligned her.

20. Cited by Strickland, *Lives of the Queens,* 5:249–50.

21. Cited in *PPM,* 3:392. J. E. Gray, "The Source of *The Emperour of the East,*" *Review of English Studies* 1 (1950):126–35; Peter G. Phialas, "The Sources of Massinger's *Emperour of the East,*" *PMLA* 65 (1950):473–82.

22. Bentley, *Stage,* 1:226–27.

Chapter Six

1. Between 1631 and 1633 Massinger had the following plays licensed for performance: *The Emperor of the East,* 11 March 1631; *Believe as You List,* 6 May 1631; *The Unfortunate Piety,* 13 June 1631; *The City Madam,* 25 May 1632. *The Fatal Dowry* played at court on 3 February 1631 and was printed in 1632, and, if *The Emperor of the East* was given at court, as its court prologue seems to indicate, then it probably played between March, when it was licensed for performance, and November, when it was licensed for publication.

2. *The Maid of Honour, The Emperor of the East,* and *The Fatal Dowry* were all first printed in 1632; *A New Way to Pay Old Debts,* in 1633; see n. 1 for four plays licensed.

3. See Bentley, *Stage,* 3:193–225. Davenant was back in London by the end of 1633; his *The Witts,* licensed under protest in January 1634, met with organized opposition from the audience; his *Love and Honour* was licensed in November 1634 and evidently played at Blackfriars; *News from Plymouth* was licensed in August 1635, and both the date of the license

and the epilogue to the play indicate that it was written for the Globe; "Epilogue, To a Vacation play at The Globe" was printed in Davenant's *Madagascar; With Other Poems* in 1638. The Globe seems an appropriate and likely place for Davenant to apologize to the popular audience. Moseley and Robinson entered *News from Plymouth* in the Stationers' Register in 1646, and the title remained Moseley's property until 1672.

    4. Cited by Bentley, *Stage,* 4:789.

    5. *Ibid,* 3:222.

    6. *Ibid,* 3:224.

    7. Philip Edwards, "Massinger and the Censor," in *Essays on Shakespeare and Elizabethan Drama,* ed. Richard Hosley (Columbia: University of Missouri Press, 1962), 341–50.

    8. Strickland, *Lives of the Queens,* 5:256, relates a similar incident, from an account by Swift, of Queen Henrietta Maria's throwing the king's gift of a diamond brooch to the floor when he accidentally stuck her as he tried to pin it on her gown. Massinger may have used a widely known illustration of the queen's childish behavior to invite the audience to associate the history of Almira with the power and possibilities of the queen.

    9. Bentley, *Stage,* 4:795.

    10. The term, or terms, signify a complex set of values and attributes that include genius, inventiveness, cleverness, high and noble birth, and, perhaps, other values or associations that have yet to be identified. Beal ("Massinger at Bay"), in his commentary to the use of the word in the manuscripts, notes the centrality of the word to the quarrel.

    11. Cited by Maidment and Logan in their Introduction to Davenant's *The Just Italian* in *The Dramatic Works of William D'Avenant* (London: Sotheran & Co., 1872), 1:202.

Chapter Seven

    1. Butler, *Theater and Crisis,* 9–11; quoted in chapter 2.

    2. *A Chain of Golden Poems,* 1658, sig N5v.

    3. J. H. P. Pafford, "A New Poem by Philip Massinger," *N&Q* 25 (1978):503–5. See also C. A. Gibson, "The New Massinger Elegy," *N&Q* 29 (1982):489–90.

Selected Bibliography

PRIMARY SOURCES

1. Independent Plays
All of the independent plays are included in the collected editions of
   Gifford and of Edwards and Gibson.
The Bashful Lover (1636). *Three New Playes*. London: for Humphrey Mose-
   ley, 1655.
Believe As You List (1631). EDITIONS: T. Crofton Croker, ed., assisted
   by F. W. Fairholt. London: for the Percy Society, 1849; J. S.
   Farmer, ed. London: Tudor Facsimile Texts, 1907; Charles J.
   Sisson, ed. Oxford: Oxford University Press for the Malone Society,
   1927.
The Bondman (1623). *The Bond-Man: An Ancient Storie*. London: Edw.
   Allde, for John Harison, 1624; second quarto, 1638. EDITIONS: Ben-
   jamin Townley Spencer, ed. Princeton: Princeton University Press,
   1932.
The City Madam (1632). *The Citty madam, A Comedie*. London: for Andrew
   Pennycuicke, 1658; another issue 1659. EDITIONS: Rudolf Kirk, ed.
   Princeton Studies in English, no. 10. Princeton: Princeton University
   Press, 1934; T. W. Craik, ed. The New Mermaids. London: Ernest
   Benn, 1964; Cyrus Hoy, ed. Regents Renaissance Drama Series.
   Lincoln: University of Nebraska Press, 1964.
The Duke of Milan (1621–1622). *The Dvke of Millaine. A Tragedie*. London:
   B. A. for Edward Blackmore, 1623. EDITIONS: Thomas Whitfield
   Baldwin, ed. Lancaster, Pa: New Era Printing, 1918.
The Emperor of the East (1631). *The Emperovr Of the East. A Tragae-Comoedie*.
   London: by Thomas Harper for John Waterson, 1632. EDITIONS: P.
   G. Phialas, ed. Ph. D., diss., Yale University, 1948.
The Great Duke of Florence (1627?). *The Great Dvke of Florence. A Comicall
   Historie*. London: for John Marriot, 1636. EDITIONS: Johanne M.
   Stochholm, ed. Baltimore: J. H. Furst, 1933.
The Guardian (1633). *The Guardian, A Comical-History* in *Three New Plays*.
   London: for Humphrey Moseley, 1655.
The Maid of Honour (1630). London: I. B. for Robert Allot, 1632. EDI-
   TIONS: Eva A. W. Bryne, ed. London: for Bryn Mawr, 1927.
A New Way to Pay Old Debts (1625?) *A New Way to Pay Old Debts A*

Comoedie. London: E. P. for Henry Seyle, 1633. EDITIONS: Brander
Matthews, ed. In *Representative English Comedies,* edited by C. M.
Gayley, vol. 3, 301–413. New York: Macmillan, 1914; A. H.
Cruickshank, ed. Oxford: Oxford University Press, 1926; Muriel St.
Clare Byrne, ed. London: Falcon Educational Books, 1949.
The Parliament of Love (1624). EDITIONS: Kathleen Marguerite Lea, checked
by W. W. Greg. Malone Society Reprints. London: for the Malone
Society, 1928.
The Picture (1629). *The Picture A Tragaecomedie.* London: I. N. for Thomas
Walkley, 1630. EDITIONS: Giles E. Dawson, ed. Ph. D. diss., Cornell
University, 1931.
The Renegado, or The Gentleman of Venice (1624). *The Renegado, A Tragae-
comedie.* London: A. M. for John Waterson, 1630. EDITIONS: Alice
Senob, ed. Ph. D. diss., University of Chicago, 1939.
The Roman Actor (1626). *The Roman Actor. A Tragaedie.* London: B. A.
and T. F. for Robert Allot, 1629. EDITIONS: Warren Lee Sandidge,
Jr., ed. Princeton Studies in English, no. 4. Princeton: Princeton
University Press, 1929.
The Unnatural Combat (1621–25?). *The Vnnatvrall Combat. A Tragedie.*
London: B. G. for John Waterson, 1639. EDITIONS: Robert Stockdale
Telfer, ed. Princeton Studies in English, no. 7. Princeton: Princeton
University Press, 1932.
A Very Woman, or The Prince of Tarent (1634). *A Very Woman, Or the Prince
of Tarent. A Tragi-Comedy* in *Three New Plays.* London: for Humphrey
Moseley, 1655.
COLLECTED EDITIONS:
The Dramatic Works of Mr. Philip Massinger, Compleat. 4 vols. Edited by
Thomas Coxeter. London, 1759.
The Dramatick Works of Philip Massinger. 4 vols. Edited by John Monck
Mason. Introductions by T. Davies and G. Colman. London, 1779.
The Plays of Philip Massinger. 4 vols. Edited by William Gifford, with an
essay by John Ferriar. London, 1805. A preferable edition, 1813.
The Dramatic Works of Massinger and Ford. Introduction by Hartley Col-
eridge. London, 1840.
*The Plays of Philip Massinger, from the Text of William Gifford, with the
Addition of the Tragedy 'Believe as You List.'* Edited by Francis Cun-
ningham. London: J. C. Hotten, 1871.
Philip Massinger. 2 vols. Edited by Arthur Symons. The Mermaid Series.
London: T. Fisher Unwin, 1887–89.
The Plays and Poems of Philip Massinger. 5 vols. Edited by Philip Edwards
and Colin Gibson. Oxford: Clarendon Press, 1976.
Selected Plays of Philip Massinger. Edited by Colin Gibson. Cambridge:
Cambridge University Press, 1978.

2. Authentic Collaborations
The Fatal Dowry (1616–19) with Nathan Field. *The Fatall Dowry: A Tragedy . . .* by P. M. and N. F. London: by John Norton for Francis Constable, 1632. EDITIONS: Included in all collected editions of Massinger; Charles Lacy Lockert, Jr., ed. Lancaster, Penn.: New Era Printing, 1918; T. A. Dunn, ed. Berkeley: University of California Press 1969; Carol Bishop, ed. Salzburg: Institüt für Englische Sprache und Literatur, Universitat Salzburg, 1976.
The Virgin Martyr (1620). *The Virgin Martir, A Tragedie.* Written by Phillip Messenger *{sic}* and Thomas Decker *{sic}*. London: by Bernard Alsop for Thomas Iones, 1622. EDITIONS: Included in all collected editions of Massinger until Edwards and Gibson; Fredson Bowers, ed. In *The Dramatic Works of Thomas Dekker*, vol. 3, 365–480. Cambridge: Cambridge University Press, 1966.

3. Assumed Collaborations
All the plays written with Fletcher are included in collected editions of the plays of Beaumont and Fletcher.
The Beggars' Bush (1622) with John Fletcher? "Beggars Bvsh" included in the Beaumont and Fletcher First Folio, 1647. EDITIONS: John H. Dorenkamp, ed. The Hague: Mouton, 1967.
The Bloody Brother, or Rollo Duke of Normandy (1617? revised 1627–30?) with John Fletcher? *The Bloody Brother. A Tragedy.* By B. J. F. London: by R. Bishop for Thomas Allott and Iohn Crook, 1639; *The Tragedy of Rollo Duke of Normandy.* Written by John Fletcher. Oxford: Leonard Lichfield, printer to the University, 1640; "The Bloody Brother; Or, Rollo. A Tragedy" included in the second Beaumont and Fletcher Folio, 1679. EDITIONS: J. D. Jump, ed. *Rollo, Duke of Normandy, or The Bloody Brother. A Tragedy. Attributed to John Fletcher, George Chapman, Ben Jonson and Philip Massinger.* Liverpool: University Press of Liverpool, 1948.
Bonduca (1609–14) with Beaumont and Fletcher? "Bondvca. A Tragedy" in Beaumont and Fletcher First Folio, 1647. EDITIONS: Walter Wilson Greg, ed. The Malone Society Reprints. Oxford: Oxford University Press for the Malone Society, 1951.
The Captain (1609–1612?) with Beaumont and Fletcher? "The Captain. A Comedy" in the Beaumont and Fletcher First Folio, 1647.
The Cure for a Cuckold (1624–25) with Webster? Rowley? *A Cure For A Cuckold. A Pleasant Comedy.* Written by John Webster and William Rowley. London, 1661. EDITIONS: F. L. Lucas, ed. In *The Complete Works of John Webster*, vol. 3, 3–118. London: Chatto & Windus, 1927.
The Custom of the Country (c. 1619–20 and 1638?) with John Fletcher?

"The Custome of the Countrey" is included in the Beaumont and Fletcher First Folio, 1647.

The Double Marriage (c. 1621) with John Fletcher? "The double Marriage" is included in the Beaumont and Fletcher First Folio, 1647.

The Elder Brother (1625) with John Fletcher? *The Elder Brother A Comedie.* Written by Iohn Fletcher, 1637; included in the second Beaumont and Fletcher Folio, 1679.

The Fair Maid of the Inn (1625/6) with John Fletcher? Included in the Beaumont and Fletcher First Folio, 1647. EDITIONS: F. L. Lucas, ed. In *The Complete Works of John Webster,* vol. 4, 147–238. London: Chatto & Windus, 1927.

The Faithful Friends (c. 1614–1621), with Beaumont and Fletcher? First included in the collected works of Beaumont and Fletcher by Weber, 1812. EDITIONS: Vivian Ridler, ed. Oxford: Oxford University Press for the Malone Society, 1975.

The False One (c. 1620) with John Fletcher? Included in the Beaumont and Fletcher First Folio, 1647.

The Honest Man's Fortune (1613) with Fletcher, Field, and Daborne? Included in the Beaumont and Fletcher First Folio, 1647. EDITIONS: Johan Gerritsen, ed. Groningen: J. B. Walters, 1952.

The Island Princess (1619–21) with Fletcher? Included in the Beaumont and Fletcher First Folio, 1647.

The Knight of Malta (1616–18) with Nathan Field and John Fletcher? Included in the Beaumont and Fletcher First Folio, 1647. EDITIONS: Marianne Brocke, ed. Ph. D. diss., Bryn Mawr, 1944.

The Laws of Candy (1619?) with Fletcher? Included in the Beaumont and Fletcher First Folio, 1647.

The Little French Lawyer (1619–1623) with John Fletcher? Included in the Beaumont and Fletcher First Folio, 1647.

The Lovers' Progress, or The Wandering Lovers, or Cleander (1623, revised 1634), Massinger's revision of Fletcher? Included in the Beaumont and Fletcher First Folio, 1647.

Love's Cure, or The Martial Maid (? and 1625?) revision of Beaumont and Fletcher? Included in the Beaumont and Fletcher First Folio, 1647.

The Old Law (1618?) with Thomas Middleton and William Rowley? *The Excellent Comedy, called The Old Law: Or a new way to please you.* By Phil. Massinger. Tho. Middleton. William Rowley. London, 1656. EDITIONS: Included in Gifford and Cunningham editions of Massinger; Catherine Shaw, ed. *The Old Law by Thomas Middleton and William Rowley.* New York: Garland Publishing, 1982.

The Prophetess (1622) with John Fletcher? Included in the Beaumont and Fletcher First Folio, 1647.

The Queen of Corinth (1616–17) with John Fletcher and Nathan Field? Included in the Beaumont and Fletcher First Folio, 1647.

The Sea Voyage (1622) with John Fletcher? Included in the Beaumont and Fletcher First Folio, 1647.

The Second Maiden's Tragedy (1611) Middleton? Massinger? EDITIONS: Vol. 1. *Old English Drama,* 1824–25; R. H. Shepherd, ed. In *The Works of George Chapman,* vol. 3. London: Chatto and Windus, 1875; W. W. Greg, ed. Malone Society Reprints. Oxford: Oxford University Press for the Malone Society, 1909; Anne Lancashire, ed. The Revels Plays. Baltimore: Johns Hopkins University Press, 1978.

Sir John van Olden Barnavelt (1619) with John Fletcher? EDITIONS: A. H. Bullen, ed. In *A Collection of Old Plays,* vol. 2. London, 1883; Wilhelmina P. Frijlinck, ed. *The Tragedy of Sir John van Olden Barnavelt.* Amsterdam: H. G. van Dorssen, 1922; London: Malone Society, 1980.

The Spanish Curate (1622) with John Fletcher? Included in the Beaumont and Fletcher First Folio, 1647.

Thierry and Theodoret (1607–1617?) with Beaumont and Fletcher? *The Tragedy of Thierry, King of France, and His Brother Theodoret.* London: for Thomas Walkley, 1621; . . . By John Fletcher. London: for Humphrey Moseley, 1648; . . . By Francis Beaumont and John Fletcher. London: for Humphrey Moseley, 1649.

COLLECTED EDITIONS:

The Dramatic Works in the Beaumont and Fletcher Canon. Edited by Fredson Bowers. 4 vols. to date. Cambridge: Cambridge University Press, 1966–79.

The Works of Francis Beaumont and John Fletcher. Edited by A. H. Bullen. 4 vols. 20 plays. Variorum edition. London: G. Bell & Sons, and A. H. Bullen, 1904–12.

The Works of Francis Beaumont and John Fletcher. Edited by Arnold Glover and A. R. Waller. 10 vols. Cambridge: Cambridge University Press, 1905–20.

The Works of Beaumont and Fletcher. Edited by Alexander Dyce. 11 vols. London: John Murray, 1843–46. Reprint. Freeport, N.Y.: Books for Libraries Press, 1970.

4. Poems

"A Charme for a Libeller" (1630). Peter Beal, "Massinger at Bay: Unpublished Verses." *Yearbook of English Studies* 10 (1980):190–203.

"A Copy of a Letter" (1615?). In *Poems consisting of Epistles & Epigrams, Satyrs, Epitaphs and Elegies, Songs and Sonnets. With variety of other drolling Verses upon several Subjects,* edited by John Eliot, 108–11. London: for Henry Brome, 1658; second edition 1661. EDITIONS: of

Dublin manuscript text: A. B. Grosart. "Literary-Finds in Trinity College, Dublin, and Elsewhere." *Englische Studien* 26 (1899): 4–6; reprinted by P. Simpson. "Two Poems of Philip Massinger." *Athenaeum* 4115 (8 September 1906):273; Cruickshank; Lawless, *Poems;* Edwards and Gibson, *The Plays and Poems of Philip Massinger.*

"A funerall Poem Sacred to the memorie of . . . Sr Warham Sentliger Knight . . ." (1631). J. H. P. Pafford. "A New Poem by Philip Massinger." *Notes and Queries* 25 (1978):503–5.

"London's Lamentable Estate" (1625). Edited by A. K. McIlwraith (1931). In *Genius, Loci and Other Essays.* Oxford: Clarendon Press, 1950; reprinted by Lawless, *Poems;* Edwards and Gibson.

"A New Year's Gift" (1621–22?). A. B. Grosart, "Literary-Finds in Trinity College, Dublin, and Elsewhere." *Englische Studien* 26 (1899):6–7; reprinted by P. Simpson, "Two Poems of Philip Massinger." *Athenaeum,* 4115 (8 September 1906):273; T. W. Baldwin, ed. *The Duke of Milan;* Cruickshank; Lawless, *Poems;* Edwards and Gibson.

"Prologue to ye Mayde of honour" (1630). Beal, Peter, "Massinger at Bay: Unpublished Verses in a War of the Theatres." *Yearbook of English Studies* 10 (1980):190–203.

"Sero, Sed Serio" (1636). In standard editions of Massinger; Lawless, *Poems;* Edwards and Gibson.

"To His Son, Upon His Minerva" (1630s). In *Wit Restored in several select Poems not formerly published,* edited by Sir John Mennes and James Smith, 142. London: for R. Pollard, N. Brooks, and T. Dring, 1658; reprinted in standard collected editions of Massinger; T. Park and E. Dubois in *Facetiae. Musarum Decliciae: or The Muses' Recreation . . . ,* 1817 (reprinted by J. C. Hotten, 1874); A. B. Grosart, "Literary-Finds in Trinity College, Dublin, and Elsewhere." *Englische Studien* 26 (1899):7; Lawless, *Poems;* Edwards and Gibson.

"To James Shirley" (1630). In *The Grateful Servant* by James Shirley, sig. 2A4. London: by Bernard Alsop and Thomas Fawcett for John Grove, 1630; second quarto 1637; reprinted in standard collected editions of Massinger; *The Dramatic Works and Poems of Shirley,* edited by Dyce and Gifford, 1833; Lawless, *Poems;* Edwards and Gibson.

"To Sir Francis Foljambe" (1623). In *The Plays of Philip Massinger,* edited by W. Gifford. 2d and 3d editions. London: 1813, 1830. Reprinted by Lawless, *Poems;* Edwards and Gibson.

"The Virgin's Character" (1625–1630?). A. K. McIlwraith, " 'The Virgins Character': A New Poem by Philip Massinger." *Review of English Studies* 4 (1928):64–68; Edwards and Gibson; reprinted by Lawless, *Poems.*

COLLECTED EDITIONS:

The Poems of Philip Massinger, with Critical Notes. Edited by Donald S. Lawless. Ball State Monograph, no. 13. Muncie, Ind.: Ball State University, 1968.

The Plays and Poems of Philip Massinger. Edited by Philip Edwards and Colin Gibson, vol. 4, 386–423. Oxford: Clarendon Press, 1976.

Secondary Sources

1. Bibliographies

Logan Terence. "Philip Massinger." In *The Later Jacobean and Caroline Dramatists: A Survey and Bibliography of Recent Studies in English Renaissance Drama,* edited by Terence P. Logan and Denzell S. Smith, 90–119. Lincoln: University of Nebraska Press, 1978.

Pennel, Charles A. and William P. Williams. *Elizabethan Bibliographies Supplements VIII.* London: Nether Press, 1968.

Tannenbaum, Samuel A. *Philip Massinger (A Concise Bibliography).* New York: for the editor, 1938; reprint, 1967, vol. 6, *Elizabethan Bibliographies.*

2. Books and Parts of Books

Baldwin, Thomas Whitfield. Introduction and Commentary in his edition of *The Duke of Milan.* Lancaster, Pa: New Era Printing, 1918. Full comparison of play with sources and other plays of the period; publication history, stage history, and critical analysis.

Ball, Robert Hamilton. *The Amazing Career of Sir Giles Overreach.* London: Oxford University Press, 1939. A full study of *A New Way to Pay Old Debts* that includes a study of sources, topical allusions, reputation and influence, and a detailed history of the play in the theater.

Barton, Anne. "The Distinctive Voice of Massinger." In *Philip Massinger: A Critical Reassessment,* edited by Douglas Howard, 231–32. Cambridge: Cambridge University Press, 1985; reprint from *TLS,* 20 May 1977, 623–24. Review of Edwards and Gibson that also reviews Massinger's canon and invites further study of that canon.

Bishop, Carol. Introduction and Notes in her *A Critical Edition of Massinger and Field's "The Fatal Dowry."* Salzburg: Institüt für Englische Sprache und Literatur, Universitat Salzburg, 1976. Analyzes play as a Herculean tragedy, revolving around a hero in conflict with a hostile environment and influenced by Massinger's "taste for forensic disputes"; lacks a revenge plot, but includes acts of personal revenge that are never condoned. Finds that the play deals with both the limitations of law and of those who administer it and seems to be more concerned with the law in practice than with abstract systems of justice. Considers the play unusually "rank conscious" and anti-bourgeois in tone.

Bryne, Eva A. W. Introduction and Notes in her edition of *The Maid of Honour*, ix–lii, 85–136. London: for Bryn Mawr, 1927. Provides literary sources and analogues, historical and political elements, a discussion of the date of the play, criticism, a textual note, and full commentary to the text.

Butler, Martin. "Romans in Britain: *The Roman Actor* and the Early Stuart Classical Play." In *Philip Massinger: A Critical Reassessment*, edited by Douglas Howard, 139–70. Cambridge: Cambridge University Press, 1985. Uses Massinger's play to illustrate the use by writers of the period of classical materials to express political opposition.

————.*Royal Slaves? The Stuart Court and the Theatres. Renaissance Drama Newsletter: Supplement Two*, 1984. Treats the relation of the Caroline court and the theater of opposition.

————.*Theatre and Crisis, 1632–1642*. London: Cambridge University Press, 1984. Historical reconsideration of the relation of theater and contemporary events, methods employed by dramatists to express opposition, and Massinger's central role in the theater of opposition.

Byrne, Muriel St. Clare. Introduction and Notes in her edition of *A New Way to Pay Old Debts*, 1–16. London: Falcon Educational Books, 1949. Focuses on theater history of the play and Hazlitt's analysis of it; examines poetry and style.

Chelli, Maurice. *Le Drame de Massinger*. Lyon: M. Audin, 1923. Full-length study in French; reprints many of the biographical documents; useful analyses of the plays, particularly in their relation to the drama of law; considers the trial and scenes modeled on legal defense central to Massinger's art.

Craik, T. W. Introduction to his edition of *The City Madam*. The New Mermaids. London: Ernest Benn, 1964. Plot summary and description of characters as subservient to plot. Points out suggestions that stage directions were for original production.

Cruickshank, A. H. *Philip Massinger*. Oxford: Oxford University Press, 1920. Brief treatment of the life and full critical treatment of the canon primarily in terms of style, imitations, and borrowings. Includes facsimiles of documents, some of the poems, and list of collaborated plays attributed to Massinger.

Dorenkamp, John H. Introduction and Commentary in his edition of *The Beggars' Bush*. The Hague: Mouton, 1967. Discusses attribution of shares, provides a critical evaluation, and reviews the reputation of the play.

Dunn, T. A. Introduction in his edition of *The Fatal Dowry*. Berkeley:

University of California Press, 1969. Focuses on the predominance of forensic rhetoric and considers forensic drama Massinger's specialty. Describes the play as a moral drama of abstractions of human relationships; loyalty and trust and their opposites form the antithetical themes of the play that centers around the idea of courtesy.

————.*Philip Massinger: The Man and the Playwright.* Edinburgh: Thomas Nelson, for the University College of Ghana, 1957. A full-length critical biography by one who seems to dislike both Massinger and his plays. Recounts most of the known facts.

Edwards, Philip. "Massinger the Censor." In *Essays on Shakespeare and Elizabethan Drama,* edited by Richard Hosley, 341–50. Columbia: University of Missouri Press, 1962. Focuses on the complex drama of moral struggle and suffering that is coexistent with plots of melodramatic and exaggerated moral choices.

————."The Royal Pretenders in Massinger and Ford." *Essays and Studies* 27 (1974):18–36. Comparison of *Believe as You List* and Ford's *Perkin Warbeck* as closely related plays that are pessimistic and hostile to Charles.

————.*Threshold of a Nation.* Cambridge: Cambridge University Press, 1979. Treats the tensions and conflicts of dramatists in a court-dependent theater particularly as they are reflected in *The Roman Actor.* Stresses the idea that nostalgic conservatives (looking back to traditional values) shared many tenets with radical opponents of the Crown.

Frijlinck, Wilhelmina. Introduction to her edition of *Sir John van Olden Barnavelt.* Amsterdam: H. G. van Dorssen, 1922. Provides the documentary accounts of the execution of Barnavelt and other source materials; discusses the censuring of the play and the subsequent alterations; evaluates the play.

Gerritsen, Johan. Introduction to his edition of *The Honest Man's Fortune,* i–xxxiv. Groningen: J. B. Walters, 1952. Particularly valuable for discussion of the handwriting that is shared by this play and other manuscript plays associated with Massinger.

Gibson, Colin. "Massinger's Theatrical Language." In *Philip Massinger, A Critical Reassessment,* edited by Douglas Howard, 9–38. Cambridge: Cambridge University Press, 1985. Illustrates that "Massingerian drama as a whole evinces . . . the coordination of theatrical and verbal imagery, and its coherence with the central conception of each play."

Goldberg, Jonathan. *James I and the Politics of Literature.* Baltimore: Johns Hopkins University Press, 1983. A radical reading of the period and its literature with a full chapter devoted to *The Roman Actor.*

Heinemann, Margot. *Puritanism and Theatre: Thomas Middleton and Opposition Drama under the Early Stuarts.* Cambridge: Cambridge University Press, 1980. Excellent treatment of opposition theater, context, and some treatment of Massinger.

Hensman, Bertha. *The Shares of Fletcher, Field and Massinger in Twelve Plays of the Beaumont and Fletcher Canon.* 2 vols. Salzburg: Institüt Für Englische Sprache und Literatur, Universitat Salzburg, 1974. Seeks to determine the attribution of shares of twelve plays by determining the sources of the plays and analyzing the selection from and characteristic use of sources; provides useful compilation of repeated patterns and elements.

Hermassi, Karen. *Polity and Theater in Historical Perspective.* Berkeley: University of California Press, 1977. Suggests many plays, like Massinger's, were "dramatized not so much to persuade the audiences to adopt some future action but to place them irrevocably before the 'facts' and trouble the course of their action in the present."

Howard, Douglas. "Massinger's Political Tragedies." In his *Philip Massinger: A Critical Reassessment,* 117–37. Cambridge: Cambridge University Press, 1985. Considers *The Roman Actor* and *Believe as You List,* both written after Fletcher's death, as illustrations of Massinger's independent, mature, tragic art.

————, ed. *Philip Massinger: A Critical Reassessment.* Cambridge: Cambridge University Press, 1985. A collection of eight new critical essays, all herein annotated, an introduction, and a reprint of Anne Barton's review of Edwards and Gibson.

Hoy, Cyrus. Introduction to his edition of *The City Madam.* Regents Renaissance Drama Series. Lincoln: University of Nebraska Press, 1964. Reviews the problem of the date in light of the prologue to *The Guardian,* discusses the comedic structure of the play, provides a history of the text, and gives a brief review of Massinger's achievements.

————. Introduction to and Commentary on *The Virgin Martyr* in his *Introductions, Notes, and Commentaries to Texts in "The Dramatic Works of Thomas Dekker,"* vol. 3, 179–231. Cambridge: Cambridge University Press, 1980. Summarizes the criticism and scholarship, attribution studies, problems, sources, and theater history for the play. Commentary provides various readings, explanations, and cross references.

————. "Massinger as Collaborator: The Plays with Fletcher and Others." In *Philip Massinger: A Critical Reassessment,* edited by Douglas Howard, 51–82. Cambridge: Cambridge University Press, 1985.

Kirk, Rudolf. Introduction and Notes in his edition of *The City Madam,* 1–63. Princeton Studies in English, no. 10. Princeton: Princeton University Press, 1934. Provides a full study of the publication history

and the stage history, discusses problem of date in light of the prologue of *The Guardian,* and analyzes and evaluates the play.

Knights, L. C. "The Significance of Massinger's Social Comedies." In his
Drama and Society in the Age of Jonson, 270–300. London: Chatto &
Windus, 1937. Considers Massinger the last of the Elizabethans,
advocating the aristocratic values of a past age but very little concerned
with the middle class or the common man.

Lancashire, Anne. Introduction to her edition of *The Second Maiden's
Tragedy,* i–xix. The Revels Plays. Baltimore: Johns Hopkins University Press, 1978. Discusses oblique methods of addressing sensitive
political and religious matters, methods that are supported by kinds
of matter excised in the manuscript; also notes influence of this play
on *The Duke of Milan.*

Lawless, Donald S. *Philip Massinger and his Associates.* Ball State Monograph, 10. Muncie, Ind.: Ball State University, 1967. Based on his
unpublished dissertation and referring back to it frequently, Lawless
presents the fullest available account of the documented records of
Massinger's life: family connections, patrons, commenders, and other
associates. Although both he and others have recovered additional
records and have revised conclusions, this is still valuable.

Leech, Clifford. *The John Fletcher Plays.* London: Chatto & Windus, 1962.
Provides critical accounts and descriptions of many of the Fletcher/
Massinger collaborations.

Leonard, Nancy S. "Overreach at Bay: Massinger's *A New Way to Pay Old
Debts."* In *Philip Massinger: A Critical Reassessment,* edited by Douglas
Howard, 171–92. Cambridge: Cambridge University Press, 1985.
Finds the play undercuts many of the values of the aristocratic characters who are ostensibly advocated by the play. Concludes that the
play is a more ironic and complex image of its age than heretofore
realized.

Lockert, Charles Lacy, Jr. Introduction and Notes in his edition of *The
Fatal Dowry.* Lancaster, Pa: New Era Printing, 1918.

McDonald, Russ. "High Seriousness and Popular Form: The Case of *The
Maid of Honour."* In *Philip Massinger, A Critical Reassessment,* edited
by Douglas Howard, 83–116. Cambridge: Cambridge University
Press, 1985. Discusses the play in terms of two central questions:
artistic independence and the relationship of idea to form.

Maxwell, Baldwin. *Studies in Beaumont, Fletcher, and Massinger.* Chapel
Hill: University of North Carolina Press, 1939. Reviews assignment
of shares and questions methods of establishing attribution. Points
out that most of Massinger's allusions from Shakespeare come after
publication of First Folio.

Neill, Michael. " 'The Tongues of Angels': Charity and the Social Order in *The City Madam.*" In *Philip Massinger: A Critical Reassessment,* edited by Douglas Howard, 193–220. A detailed analysis of the play in relation to the religious texts that define the charity that is central, in its absence, to the play.

Parker, Henerie. "To his hono:d frend Mr. Phillip Massinger, having not that iust applause for one of his plays wch was due him." In *A Little Ark: Containing Sundry Pieces of Seventeenth-Century Verse,* edited by G. Thorn-Drury, 2. London: P. J. & A. E. Dobell, 1921. Probably written on the occasion of *Emperor of the East* that seems to have met with audience opposition. Reprinted in Dunn, *Philip Massinger: The Man and the Playwright.* Edinburgh: Thomas Nelson, for the University of Ghana, 1957.

Ridler, Vivian. Introduction to her edition of *The Faithful Friends,* i–xx. Discusses the various hands, one of which may be Massinger's, involved in the manuscript of the play, the evidence of self-censorship of political allusions in the alterations, and evidence of a Caroline revival.

Sandidge, Warren Lee, Jr. Introduction and Commentary in his edition of *The Roman Actor.* Princeton Studies in English, no. 4. Princeton: Princeton University Press, 1929. Full treatment of sources, including sources for the plays within the play, history of publication and performances, and a critical analysis of the play.

Spencer, Benjamin Townley. Introduction and Notes to his edition of *The Bondman,* 1–74, 161–256. Princeton: Princeton University Press, 1932. Provides a bibliography of editions and reprints, stage history, study of sources, detailed account of relation of play to both contemporary events and classical ideas, an estimate of the play, and commentary to individual lines.

————. "Philip Massinger." In *Seventeenth Century Studies by Members of the Graduate School, University of Cincinnati,* edited by Robert Shafer, 3–119. Princeton: Princeton University Press, 1933. Treats Massinger's social and political views at length and concludes that he was an aristocrat at heart and resented the encroaching middle class.

Stochholm, Johanne M. Introduction and Commentary in her edition of *The Great Duke of Florence.* Baltimore: J. H. Furst, 1933. Dates the play between 1623 and 1625 on the basis of political allusions; treats sources, history of the text; and provides a critical analysis of the play.

Telfer, Robert Stockdale. Introduction and Notes in his edition of *The Unnatural Combat.* Princeton Studies in English, no. 7. Princeton: Princeton University Press, 1932. Discusses problem of dating the play, compares play elements with other plays of the period, speculates about the sources, and provides criticism and commentary.

Waith, E. M. *The Pattern of Tragicomedy in Beaumont and Fletcher.* New Haven: Yale University Press, 1952. Full study of most of the plays Massinger shared with Fletcher, both in terms of adherence to and deviation from a tragicomic pattern.

3. Articles

Alsop, J. D. "Further Connections of Sir Warham St. Leger." *Notes & Queries* 30 (1983):423. Points out family connections with Sir Richard Baker, Thomas and Robert Sackville, earls of Dorset, Samuel, Reginald, and Richard Argall, and other Kentish families.

Bennet, A. L. "The Moral Tone of Massinger's Drama." *Papers on Language and Literature* 2 (1966):207–16. Considers Massinger strongest in dramatizing moral or political issues and weakest in dramatizing romantic elements.

Burelbach, Frederick, Jr. "*A New Way to Pay Old Debts:* A Jacobean Morality." *College Language Association Journal* 12 (1969):205–13. Treats the play as a dramatized warning to Charles to avoid the Jacobean ills of ingratitude and giving power into the hands of upstarts.

Clubb, Louise George. "*The Virgin Martyr* and the *Tragedia Sacra.*" *Renaissance Drama* 7 (1964):103–26. Argues that *The Virgin Martyr* may be properly termed an English *tragedia sacre,* a genre that developed on the Continent as a by-product of the Counter-Reformation, and that Massinger with greater connections with popery than Dekker made the selection of material.

Davison, Peter H. "The Theme and Structure of *The Roman Actor.*" *Journal of the Australasian Universities Language and Literature Association* 19 (1963):39–56. Stresses the unity of the structural development of the conflict between power and human weakness in the use of state and stage.

Edwards, Philip. "The Sources of Massinger's *The Bondman.*" *Review of English Studies* 15 (1964):21–26. Discusses the classical sources, stresses the moral themes, and discounts importance of the topical allusions.

Eliot, T. S. "Philip Massinger." *TLS,* 27 May 1920, 325–26. To be read only after having read Massinger and formed one's own judgment; important in the history of Massinger's reputation.

Fothergill, Robert A. "The Dramatic Experience of Massinger's *The City Madam* and *A New Way to Pay Old Debts.*" *University of Toronto Quarterly* 43 (1973):68–86. Finds the dramatic experience confining and the plays little more than social tracts by a grave conservative.

Gardiner, Samuel Rawson. "The Political Element in Massinger." *New Shakespere Society's Transactions,* 1st ser., no. 4 (1875–76):316–19.

Traces allusions to contemporary political events and Massinger's reaction to those events through many of the plays.

Gibson, C. A. "Massinger's Hungarian History." *Yearbook of English Studies* 2 (1972):89–92. A source study and analysis for *The Picture*.

————. "Massinger's Use of His Sources for *The Roman Actor.*" *Journal of the Australasian Universities Language and Literature Association* 15 (1961):60–72. Identifies the multiple sources of the play and analyzes their use.

————. " 'The Louse's Peregrination' and the Date of *A New Way to Pay Old Debts.*" *Notes & Queries* 30 (1983):428–29. Additional evidence for fixing date as 1625.

Gill, Roma. "Collaborations and Revision in Massinger's *A Very Woman.*" *Review of English Studies* 18 (1967):136–48. Compares play with its sources; reconstructs an early version by Fletcher and Massinger; considers final version a flawed revision by Massinger.

————. "Massinger's *Believe as You List.*" *English Studies* 46 (1965):407–17. Considers Massinger a man of "limited imagination" who found all his inspiration in earlier books ("had not only read Machiavelli's work, but had also given it serious and comparatively unbiased consideration"). Considers the play a "problem play," but a fine one that raises unsolved questions about the conflict of ideologies.

Gross, Allen. "Contemporary Politics in Massinger." *Studies in English Literature* 6 (1966):279–90. Begins as an attack on those who have originated and perpetuated the "received opinion that Massinger's plays are full of specific references to contemporary politics," but then concludes that Massinger was a partially frustrated topical writer with an unflagging interest in general political theory and one able on occasion to attack particular problems.

Hogan, A. P. "The Imagery of Acting in *The Roman Actor.*" *Modern Language Review* 66 (1971):273–81. Illustrates the thematic effectiveness of the use of actors, acting, and plays.

Hoy, Cyrus. "The Shares of Fletcher and his Collaborators in the Beaumont and Fletcher Canon." *Studies in Bibliography* 8 (1956):129–46; 9 (1957):143–62; 11 (1958):85–106; 12 (1959):91–116; 13 (1960):77–108; 14 (1961):45–63; 15 (1962):71–90. Assigns shares on the basis of linguistic mannerisms; most widely accepted assignment of shares. Reviews and provides bibliography for earlier attribution studies.

————."Verbal Formulae in the Plays of Philip Massinger." *Studies in Philology* 56 (1959):600–18. Lists and discusses repeated patterns in Massinger's plays and plays he shared with others.

Huebert, Ronald. " 'An Artificial Way to Grieve': The Forsaken Woman in Beaumont and Fletcher, Massinger and Ford." *English Literary*

History 44 (1977):601–21. Comparative treatment of a single element.

Lawrence, W. J. "*The Renegado.*" *TLS,* 24 October 1929, 846. Notes transcription of play in Rawlinson's collection of manuscripts and speculates that it was prepared for a 1662 revival of the play.

McManaway, James G. "Philip Massinger and the Restoration Drama." *English Literary History* 1 (1934):276–304. Considers which plays were played, which adapted, and offers a critical evaluation of Massinger.

Mullany, Peter F. "Massinger's *The Renegado:* Religion in Stuart Tragicomedy." *Genre* 5 (1972):138–52. Finds that in the works of Massinger, Fletcher, and their collaborators, religion is divorced from the real world and becomes part of the artifice that seeks to move audiences rather than to inform them.

———. "Religion in Massinger and Dekker's *The Virgin Martyr.*" *Kosmos* 2 (1970):89–97. Concludes that religion is not used seriously within the play, but is merely a tragicomic means of entertaining.

———. "Religion in Massinger's *The Maid of Honour.*" *Renaissance Drama* 2 (1969):143–56. Finds the religion in the play artificial and merely a means to create theatrical excitement.

Neill, Michael. "Massinger Patriarchy: The Social Vision of *A New Way to Pay Old Debts.*" *Renaissance Drama* 10 (1979):185–213. Treats the play as a social document that defends the patriarchal and aristocratic values of birth and blood against the encroachments of the middle class.

Thomson, Patricia. "The Old Way and the New Way in Dekker and Massinger." *Modern Language Review* 51 (1956):168–78. Contrasts the values dramatized in *A New Way to Pay Old Debts* and in Dekker's *Shoemaker's Holiday* and concludes that while the two playwrights hold the same values, Massinger finds them seriously threatened; Dekker's play represents the Elizabethan order, Massinger's the Jacobean.

———. "World Stage in Massinger's *Roman Actor.*" *Neophilologus* 54 (1970):409–26. Illustrates the unity of theme and structure, particularly in the values represented by the major characters.

Thorssen, M. J. "Massinger's Use of *Othello* in *The Duke of Milan.*" *Studies in English Literature* 19 (1978):313–26. Develops a comparison that is made frequently.

Waith, E. M. "*Controversia* in the English Drama: Medwall and Massinger." *PMLA* 68 (1953):286–303. Isolates and describes the use of one of Massinger's most important sources.

Warner, Sir George. "An Autograph Play of Philip Massinger." *Athenaeum* 3821 (19 Jan 1901):90–91. Identifies the various hands in the autograph manuscript of *Believe as You List.*

Index

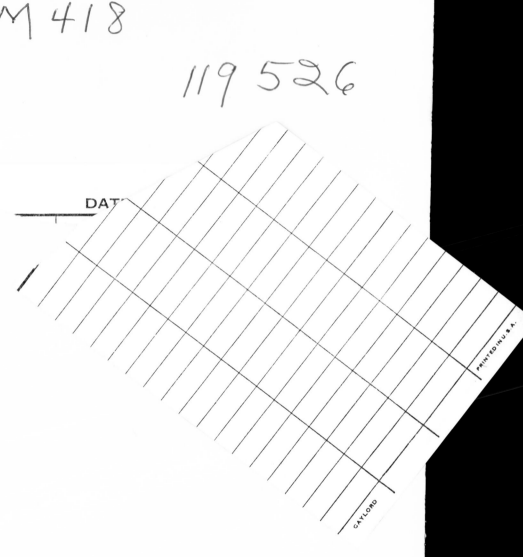